SRI RAMANUJA'S TEACHINGS *[CONTD]*

WITH

SRIVACHANA BHUSHANAM

AND

POWER OF SAGES

SRI RAMANUJA'S TEACHINGS *[CONTD]*

WITH

SRIVACHANA BHUSHANAM

AND

POWER OF SAGES

R. V. RAGHAVAN

KALPAZ

Published by

Kalpaz Publications
C-30, Satyawati Nagar,
Delhi – 110052
Ph.: 011-47034999, 9811692060
www.kalpazpublications.com
E-mail: kalpaz@hotmail.com

Distribution Network
gyanbooks.com
India, USA, Canada, UK, Australia, France

ISBN: 978-93-5722-413-0 (HB)
First Published, 2025

Printed at: Gyan Press, Delhi.

SRI RAMANUJA'S TEACHINGS
Author: R. V. RAGHAVAN

CONTENT

INTRODUCTION

In the book "Science and puranas with Sri Ramanuja's Gita bhashyam and prescribed conduct to attain liberation", only one of Sri Ramanuja's nine teachings, namely Gita bhashyam was given. In this book the remaining teachings of Sri Ramanuja, including Sri Bhashyam, which is based on sage Vyasa's brahmasutras is given. In these works, the soul's nature as well as its relationship with the body and the supersoul, otherwise called as Brahman is highlighted. The path of the soul upon death to other worlds, depending on one's karma or works, is also brought about.

In Srivacanabhushanam, the Goddess acting as a mediator between the soul and the Lord and the importance of Prapatti or surrendering oneself at the Lord is highlighted. Further it is held that a true devotee is not determined by caste, family etc. but is based solely on his relationship with the Lord.

In the power of sages, the extraordinary powers of sages of ancient times is given.

Finally, the 108 divya deshams [divine places of worship], which every Vaishnava [worshippers of Lord Narayana] must visit in his lifetime, along with its location is given.

This book is dedicated to my parents Sri K V Rajagopala Iyengar and Smt R Rukmani.

R. V. Raghavan

TEACHINGS OF SRI RAMANUJA

CHAPTER - 1

VEDANTA DEEPA

Brahman is the cause of the Universe, different from the liberated and bonded selves, as well as Prakriti [primordial matter]. When a bonded self attains liberation, he will enjoy supreme bliss, equal to that of the Supreme Brahman and not found in the Jivatman [individual self]. Though the liberated self has equal powers, as that of the Supreme Brahman in Vaikunta [abode of Brahman], he will not be able to undertake works like creation, which work is done by the Supreme Brahman. The Supreme Brahman, who is the ruler of all entities and is of the size of thumb, resides in a small space, in the lotus of the heart. People who meditate on the Supreme Brahman by Gayatri verses, Omkara etc. will attain liberation, thereby having free access in all the worlds. Such people discard both joys and sorrows. The Supreme Brahman is the ruler of Gods like Agni [God of fire], Vayu [Wind God], Surya [Sun God], etc.

The light [splendor] that shines above heaven, is the light of the Supreme Brahman [Quarter of that light is found in the Jivatman]. The terms Akasa [ether] and Prana [vital air] denote Brahman, as they are spoken of as being omniscient and the cause of creation and dissolution of the Universe [which work is done by the Supreme Brahman].

The individual self with their karmas [works], having existed since times immemorial, experience the fruits of karma. However, the Supreme Brahman, who is different from the individual self, is not subject to joys and sorrows, as He is not bound by karma. The Supreme Brahman is smaller than the smallest [as He resides in a small space in the lotus of the heart] and greater than the greatest [as He is the Universe itself]. The terms like Vaisvanara [gastric fire] and Bhuma [earth] denotes Brahman, as he is described to have the Universe for his body, comprising sentient and non-sentient beings, has supreme bliss, is immortal and is the cause of origin of all entities.

Gods who take different bodies [as they are present in the sacrifices performed simultaneously], as also the Vasus, are also qualified for meditation on Brahman. The Supreme Brahman is spoken of as Indra [Indra represent a class of beings, as after the period of one Indra, another takes over], as He has Indra for his body, being present in his self.

The matter with sentient and non-sentient beings, present in the subtle state in the body of Brahman, during dissolution, manifests as the gross state from the body of Brahman, during creation. The omniscient and omnipotent Brahman is the instrumental and material cause of the Universe.

The Vedanta [knowledge of Brahman and Atman], propounded by sage Kapila, that Pradhana is the cause of the Universe cannot be accepted, as Manu and others have comprehended the Supreme Brahman, as the cause of the Universe and the perception of sage Kapila is due to illusion. Similarly the Yoga Smriti, which describes Hiranyagarbha [Lord Brahma] not having Brahman as self, as the material cause of the Universe, cannot be accepted, as it is opposed to the teaching of the veda. [collection of hymns or prayer forming religious texts]

As the Supreme Brahman is the cause and effect of the Universe, the world being the effect of Brahman, is non-different from Brahman.

Brahman creates the world without any instrumental aid [just as milk is converted to curds], by His will alone, for His own sport.

Paramatman or Supreme Brahman is spoken of as Hiranyagarbha [seen in the orb of the sun] and the one, eternally stationed in the eye.

Pradhana or matter, being an unconscious entity, in the absence of knowership, cannot be the cause of the world, unless it is presided by conscious Brahman.

The atomic theory is rejected by believers in veda, due to qualities like non-eternity [atoms break due to radioactive decay], and absence of karma..

Avidya or ignorance cannot be the cause of the world, as ignorance is not permanent in the eternal self.

Originating from nothingness never happen [For making jar, mud is required], as also any originated thing, cannot pass into nothingness Similarly when an entity has perished, the attributes of such entities or substances are not seen anywhere, passing over into another thing. [water molecule formed by a combination of hydrogen and oxygen atoms with the properties of water being different from hydrogen and oxygen]. Hence this theory is rejected.

It is impossible to assume mutually opposite characteristics, such as being and non-being in the same substance at the same time, as it is impossible to attribute shadow and light in the same entity, at once. Therefore, the view of the Jainas, that different characteristics exist in the same object, is not tenable.

The doctrine of Pashupati is rejected as it does not establish the rulership of Ishwara or Lord. The Pancharatra Agamana is authoritative as it doesn't speak about the origin of Jiva. Similarly Pancharatra Agamana, which speaks about Sankarshana as the nature of Brahman, which in coordination with Jivatma, is the cause of origination of mind,vital force and sense organs is compatible..

The origination of Ether, Tejas and other entities, are directly from Supreme Brahman alone, as the scriptural texts declare that all entities are the bodies of Brahman. However, there is impossibility of origination for the Supreme Brahman, as He is different from all other things.

The statement of immortality of Akasa [Ether] in Chandogya Upanishad, is meant to point out, that it continues to exist for a long time like Gods.

The individual self is the knower, having consciousness as the prime attribute, is as per the scriptures. [both in the states of bondage and liberation]. The small form of the Jivatman, at the time of liberation is permanent and not subject to changes. As passing out of the body, moving to other worlds and returning to this world from there, are declared by the scriptural texts, the Jivatman is atomic in size and hence not visible to naked eyes. The Atman of the size of the atom, experiences happiness etc that extend over the whole body, just as a drop of sandal ointment, causes delight all over the body, even though it exists on a particular part of the body. The Atman abides in the heart[1] as declared from the Srutis. The Atman pervades the whole body by means of attribute of consciousness, just like the sun. Knowledge is an essential attribute of Atman, which manifests itself in waking states and is unmanifested in the states of deep sleep and others. Knowledge alone is the cause of consciousness and non-consciousness. As the Jivatman takes the sense organs and moves about as he pleases in the body, he is the doer. i.e. the Jivatman acts as per his wishes . The doership of the Jivatman is dependant upon Paramatman [Supreme Self] alone, as per the scriptural texts. The Jivatman becomes liable to get punishments or favour, as per his acts. The Jivatman is dominated by Karma and the Paramatman, being the controller and ruler of all beings, is the dispenser of the fruits of Karma. Hence the Jiva is part of Paramatman, who is omniscient and blemishless. The permission to recite vedas to a few, is because of their association with body. [though individual selves are equal]. As the Jivatmans are different from one another, on account of karma and each of them is atomic, residing in a separate body, limited to such bodies, there is no mixing up of experience.

Individual self has no origination. However Indriyas or sense organs are originated as per the scriptural texts. Paramatman alone existed prior to creation. As per the scriptural statements, there are 11 sense organs [5 each of knowledge and action and the mind]. The Indriyas or sense organs are atomic and they are imperceivable as per the Upanishads [religious text of Hinduism]. Prana or vital air, supporting the body and sense organs, is an instrument of Atman, just like eye etc. The Prana has five fold functions and they are designated as Prana, Apana, Udana, Vyana, and Samana. Prana is main air passing through the nose, Apana is air passing through the rectum as evacuated bodily air, Samana is air which adjusts the food stuff within the stomach, Udana is air passing through the throat, the stoppage of which causes suffocation and Vyana is is total air that circulates throughout the entire body]. The vital air is also minute or subtle, just like the sense organs as per the Upanishadic text. The distinctive function of Prana continues, even when the Indriyas have ceased to function. The individual creation comprising of names and forms is by Paramatman alone, as the origination of four-faced Brahma, was only after the creation of cosmic egg, comprising of fire, water and food, which comprises the earth. Thus, the formation of individual creation is by Paramatman alone, having four-faced Brahma, as his body. The ultimate goal of life is to serve the auspicious feet of Paramatman, who is the cause of the Universe, associated with Goddess Mahalakshmi, residing at Vaikunta. Philosophy of Upanishads, with copious reference to Smrutis and Sruthis, have been brought about by Sri Ramanuja. Sri Ramanuja stresses the knowledge of karma for Brahmopasana [knowledge of Brahman]. Meditation is the spiritual discipline for attaining liberation.

When the Jivatman departs, sense organs, mind along with Prana, supported by subtle elements also departs. Those people who perform mere sacrifices etc and who do not know the self, become means of enjoyment for the Gods. Persons, by virtue of good conduct [like performing sacrifices, giving charity, performing humanitarian deeds etc] go by the path of smoke through moon to heaven and pitruloka [in subtle form] and return with the residual karma [karma that remain over and above that has been experienced], to be born in various classes of humans. Persons with evil conduct [balance of bad karmas] are born as dogs, pigs and mean persons.

Those who meditate upon Brahman with faith and austerity, attain the path of Agni or Archis. For sinners there is neither attainment of Brahman nor moon, as they are bereft of good deeds. Upon descent from moon,the souls attain the state of similarity with Akasha [Ether], cloud, rain, corn, rice etc. [without staying there for long] and having reached the womb[2], there is attainment of body, from where joy and sorrow is experienced.

The creator of objects seen in dreams is the Supreme Self alone. Further a person who has united with Brahman in deep sleep, wakes up from Brahman for functioning again. The act of swooning is not considered as death, due to the presence of subtle prana, in the swooning state. Though the Supreme Brahman enjoys the bliss of sport of ruling over all other entities, as the internal self, there is no taint of any imperfection or defect like the Jivatman [on account of karma].

The Jivatman as well as Pradhana [matter], forms part of Brahman. There is no one higher than Lord Narayana, who resides in the vast Garbhodaka ocean. The Supreme Brahman is the bestower of all fruits like liberation, worldly enjoyments etc, for those who meditate on Brahman. The qualities of Brahman like knowledge, bliss etc are to be included while meditating on Brahman. Prana or vital air is to be meditated, as characterised by the qualities of being the eldest and most celebrated and as water constitute garment for Prana, a meditator upon Prana should sip little water before and after eating food. The Paramatman residing in Aditya Mandal [orb of sun] and the right eye should be meditated separately. A person who attains a subtle body [on destruction of good and evil deeds], meditating upon Paramatman, travels through the path of Devayana or Archiradi Marg.

Further the qualities of Brahman like neither massive nor atomic is to be combined in all kinds of meditations, just like the quality of bliss of Brahman. Those who depart from the world, realising the Atman and reflecting upon his auspicious qualities will have free movement in all the worlds. Further the form of meditation of the one who is in Akasha [Ether], as well as in the heart of all beings, is the same as He is having attributes of true will, true desire, ruler of all beings etc. One should meditate on the syllable "OM"[3], as it is more powerful and different from fruits such as "Swarga" [heaven].

[The meditation dependent upon Udgitha or uttering the sacred syllable "OM" is to be practiced optionally, as it has a different fruit from the fruit of sacrifice]. Knowers of Brahman should perform karma without any desire for fruit thereof.

The meditation upon Paramatman is to be repeated. The object of meditation in all Brahmavidyas, is the Supreme Brahman or Narayana. As the Paramatman, the object of meditation, is the inner self of the Jivatman, the essential nature of Jivatman [different from that in the state of bondage], ,is also included in the object of meditation. Just as the meditation of branches of Veda relate to all branches of the veda, the mantra [prayer] to accessories to sacrifice, relate to all branches. The Supreme Brahman is to be meditated as a whole and not in separate parts. Only one mode of meditation may be chosen, as the object of attaining Brahman is the same. For a householder, meditation or vidya [knowledge of Vedanta, which is knowledge of Brahman and atman], is in need of all rites [karma]. Hence vidya is not an accessory to karma. Moreover the karmas of a person gets destroyed, when Paramatman is realised. Further Brahmavidya [knowledge of Absolute] is seen to exist in the life of celibates. This shows that vidya is not an accessory to karma.

For a knower of ultimate reality, scriptures declare permission to eat all foods, only when there is danger to life. Even in respect of those who are outside the Ashramas or stages of life such as widowers, there is competency for Brahmavidya. However, perpetual celibates, who have fallen from their Ashrama, are not qualified for Brahmavidya. The meditation on Udgitha [uttering the sacred syllable "OM"] should be performed by the priest and not the sacrificer. For a person who is observing meditation, Manana or reflection and Mouna [silence] or peace of mind is enjoined for successful fulfillment of vidya. A knower of vidya should not reveal his greatness, just as a child does not reveal his noble parentage. For a person who meditates, there is no definite determination of time for fruits, either for worldly prosperity or for liberation. Mind and symbols should be meditated having the view of Brahman one should have the view of Aditya [Sun-God] in Udgita, because Gods like Aditya are more celebrated. Meditation, should be practised being seated, where concentration of mind becomes possible. A person attains Brahman after exhausting good and bad deeds i.e. only those good or bad deeds that have not begun to yield fruits, gets destroyed. Those that have begun to yield fruits, last till the fall of final body. At the time of death, the essential nature of sense of speech, unites with the mind. The mind with all the sense organs, unites with Prana [vital air]. Prana associated with all the subtle elements like sound, touch, form, taste and smell, in turn unites with the Jivatman, which in turn unites with the elements.

Though the passing out of the body is common to both the knower of vidya and non-knower of vidya, the knower of vidya attains Brahman passing through the Murdhanya Nadi, which is the 101st on the path of Archiradi, to attain and unite with the Brahman, accompanied by a subtle body and Prana. Non-meditators pass through other blood vessels. The Jivatman uniting with Paramatman [Brahman], is different from the union at the time of pralaya or dissolution. [It is in the form of non-separation]. The departed Atman of a man of Vidya, will follow the rays of the sun. Even though a man of vidya dies during nights, he will follow the rays of the sun, as subtle rays of the sun in the night as heat, is experienced during summer nights. The censure in respect of death during nights, relate to those who are without vidya. Similarly meditators, who die during Dakshinayana [southern course of the sun], attain Brahman after resting in the moon. A man of vidya reaches deities of lightetc [Refer Sri Bhashyam-3] Badarayana [Veda Vyasa], opines that the escorting deities lead those who meditate on Brahman and those who meditate on Pratyagatman ie pure individual self, freed from Prakriti and having Brahman as its inner self, on the path of Archiradi. [Archis meaning fire]. On attaining Brahman, the liberated self manifests his true nature, which was clouded in the state of bondage. Badarayana is of the view that the liberated self, apart from having consciousness, is devoid of all sins.

The liberated self attains whatever he wants [relatives etc], solely by his will, on account of the grace of the Paramatman. Similarly the liberated self can have a body and Indriyas as in the waking state and may also not have a body and Indriyas, according to his true will. [as in a dream state]. In the presence of the body, the liberated self, who is omniscient, attains his ancestors etc. by his mere will and experiences the joy of playing through them, as in the waking state. When the liberated self has many bodies, the self pervades them through "Dharmabhuta Jnana" or attributive consciousness, which is like luminousity of lamp. The liberated self will have all the glory of the Paramatman, except in activity relating to creation, sustenance and destruction of the Universe. He moves in all the worlds created by Brahman, enjoying in those worlds, according to his will, but he does not rule over all these things. The scriptures say that there is no return of the liberated soul, who attains Brahman, through Archiradi path to this world. Therefore, death or separation from the body, is not a solution for getting rid of karma.

END NOTES

1. The self leaves the body only at the time of death.
2. As per Srimad Bhagavatam 3.31.3, by the end of three months, genital organs appear. As per medical science, both the male and female foetus, have the same rudimentary and sexual organs for the first eight weeks of life. The harmones of mother control their development. After this, the foetus begins to produce its own harmones and by the twelfth week male and female foetus start to appear, physically different, within the womb.
3. Pranava OM- Aum describes Brahman's form as creator [Brahma], protector [Vishnu], and killer [Shiva]. It also represents the three Vedas Rig, Yajur and Sama. It also denotes the servitude of the individual self to the Supreme Self.

CHAPTER - 2

VEDANTA SARA

For a person who has completed the study of the Vedas, the first duty is to make an inquiry into works, relating to action like sacrifices etc.. Vedanta, which is a small portion of the Vedas, can give only results which are temporary, while Brahman realisation can produce eternal results. The desire to know Brahman arises in a person who wants to attain Moksha or final release. The Guru or teacher who is learned in the Vedas, should speak of the knowledge of Brahman to his pupil. Childhood, youth, old age etc. are faults attached to the body, which does not touch self. Similarly pleasure etc are closely attached to the self and does not touch the body. He, who is firmly devoted to truth obtains final release.

Prakriti [unmanifested matter in subtle state], which consists of three qualities-Saatva, Rajas and Tamas [Goodness, Passion and Ignorance], cannot produce the sentient being and this Pradhana cannot obtain knowledge of sentient and non-sentient beings. Hence a person devoted to Pradhana cannot obtain final release. The individual self's acquisition of bliss takes place, ,when he is in association with Brahman, where there is supreme bliss. The attributes of the Supreme Brahman is His unlimited Lordship over the worlds, without being under the influence of karma and not subject to modification of Prakriti [Sattva, Rajas and Tamas]. The scriptural texts declare Brahman as real, which cannot be perceived by the eye but only by a pure mind. As the scriptural texts declare that Brahman is the self and ruler of the sun, He is greater than the Gods. As the Supreme Brahman [Narayana], dwells in individual selves, all worlds and beings as well as Vedas and sacrifices, He is greater than all those mentioned. Hence Narayana, who is different from Pradhana and the individual selves, rules the worlds. The Supreme Person is meditated as Gayatri, Prana etc. Brahman is spoken as Indra in some texts. Purushasukta mentions the highest person to be the cause of the world. An aspirant for Mukti [liberation] desires to reach the place of Vishnu, which is higher than the world of Prakriti and which is beyond the path of Samsara [cycle of worldly existence]. Brahman is spoken of as the one who dwells within the eye and at the same time rules over the eye.

The individual self does not know the Supreme Brahman, who is residing within him and rules over him. The individual self is different from Pradhana, while Brahman is different from the individual self. The highest Self should be meditated in the body of the devotee at the time of Pranahuti [offering to Prana or life breath]. The Supreme Person is born as and when He desires, on account of the love he bears towards his dependents. The Supreme Brahman, with qualities of being immortal and fearless, is to be meditated with the syllable "OM". Brahman has the power to grant the individual self, his essential nature. Existent and non-existent things were created by the guidance of Veda, which is eternal and which was handed by the Supreme Brahman to four-faced Brahma, who created the worlds in the same form as it was before deluge with Brahman as his self.

Persons born in the fourth varna as per puranas [Varna was considered to be division of society on the basis of occupation in ancient India], are not entitled to Brahmavidya, initiation of thread ceremony and study of vedas.

In the state of deep sleep and death, the individual self is ignorant, unlike the Supreme Self. Hence there is distinction.

Prakriti is spoken as having light [denoting Supreme Brahman] for its origin. Hence unmanifested Prakriti [in subtle state] cannot be the cause of the world. The spiritual texts mention the unborn one, who is red,white and black in colour, producing many creatures, which cannot be Prakriti. Sun etc assume subtle form at the time of deluge and regains its original form at the time of creation. Moreover Brahman takes number of forms, which cannot be Prakriti. As Brahman is said to be the support of Prakriti, He is different from Prakriti. As it is mentioned in the scriptures that the Self [denoting Brahman], who had neither name nor form in the subtle state and was alone, thought of creating the worlds in the gross state, it is held that Prakriti is not the cause of creation. The qualities of being omniscient, existing in ether, as well as in the heart and the one to be attained is unique to the Brahman. Though Brahman assumes various forms [sentient and non-sentient beings], He is different from the objects created. For example, Stone. Similarly Brahman is different from the individual self and Prakriti. Just as a mansion is built by a person, who knows how to build them [cannot be built by a non-sentient being], Pradhana a non-sentient being, unless guided by an intelligent person [Self or Brahman], cannot be the cause of the world. The creation of world takes place due to mixture of Gunas [qualities of matter] in different proportions. However, during deluge [pralaya], the three Gunas are in a state of equilibrium. Hence creation does not take place.

The combination of atoms as the cause of creation is not tenable, as there is no motion in atoms [Atoms vibrate but do not move past one another]. Moreover since atoms have the character of non-eternity, they cannot be the cause of creation.

The theory of Buddhists that earth is produced by atoms, which in turn produces the body, is rejected, due to momentariness of all things. [things which are aggregate getting destroyed the next moment]. [atoms decay at random time].

Nescience [lack of knowledge] cannot be the cause as desire, aversion etc cannot exist in a person permanently.

The theory of origination is not accepted, because when a subsequent substance is originated, the previous ones get destroyed and the thing produced will be of nature of negation. [hydrogen combining with oxygen to form water].

Theory of nothingness is not accepted, as a thing cannot be produced by nothing.

Existence and non-existence, permanence and non-permanence, separateness and non-separateness cannot exist simultaneously. Hence Jaina philosophy is rejected.

Theory of Pasupati, which states that Pasupati is the instrumental and not the material cause is rejected, as it is against the vedic principles. [pot made from mud by a potter-mud, being the material cause and potter the instrumental cause and the pot, constituting the world of sentient and non-sentient beings]. Similarly the Lord being the agent of Pradhana, is not accepted.

Though Brahman is the cause of origin of the world, He takes incarnations, out of His own will. Prakriti and individual self are inseparable.

The individual self has knowledge, both in the state of bondage and Mukti [final release]. The self experiences happiness by pervading the whole body, through knowledge, which is his attribute. However, the knowledge which exists in the self, is absent in the state of deep sleep and manifests in waking state. This knowledge is produced when the self is in contact with the mind. Besides being the knower, the self is also the doer of actions. Scriptural texts mention that the self is active in taking the senses[1] and is moving around in his own body, according to his will and pleasure. Had

Prakriti been the doer, he must have enjoyed the fruits of action, which is not the case. The highest Self [Brahman], taking into account the individual soul's effort resulting in activity or abstinence, aids the individual selves by granting this permission. The individual self forms part of the Brahman.

Bhagavad Gita [chapter 15 verse 7] says "The individual self is an eternal part of Myself". Though the individual self is a part of the highest Self [Brahman], Brahman's characteristics are different from the individual self, as He is always free from faults, all-knowing and is possessed of true will.

Though all the selves form part of Brahman, permission to study vedas,is meant for only a few [holy men], due to connection with the body. Knowledge, happiness etc vary from self to self. Prana [vital air], which has five-fold functions, is a different form of wind. The gross elements [Ether, Air, Fire, Water and Earth] along with the individual selves, control the sense organs, due to the will of the Brahman. After creating the egg-shaped Universe of golden colour [Due to ageing stars, colour of the Universe appear as a reddish hue and gold in its purest form is reddish yellow in colour], out of fire, water and food [which comprise the earth], four-faced Brahma was created.

Flesh and mind are mostly earthly by nature, blood and prana are mostly watery by nature and marrow and bones are mostly having fire by nature. Those who perform evil actions experience the result of their karmas, in the kingdom of Yama,where there are hells. Three kinds of beings originate, one by egg, one by living being and the other which springs suddenly [including sweat], as in the case of Draupadi. The bondage and liberation of the individual self is due to the Lord's will. In all the states [waking, deep sleep etc], no imperfection arises to the highest Self [Brahman], as He is free from evil qualities and possesses all good qualities. However, the imperfection affect the individual selves. Thus, we find different characteristics in the supreme Self and the individual self, though they are found in the same body.

When an individual commits evil deeds, it incurs the displeasure of the Lord and it causes pains. The pains could be got rid of by the affection of the Lord, gained through meditation. Brahman as well as the worshipper, get pleased by uninterrupted meditation, by which the essential nature of Brahman is apprehended. The Lord bestows reward, being pleased with the worship and meditation. Other deities bestow rewards, as they have the Lord for their self. Each of the Upasanas [meditations] though taught in different texts, is one and the same. This is similar to the case of works, prescribed in vedic texts. Meditation being one and the same, there is combination of qualities, on account of non-difference of purpose. Knowledge and bliss which are the essential characteristics of Brahman, have to be included in all vidyas, relating to the highest Self [Brahman]. The highest self from whom originated the spatial ether, is referred by the term "Atman" or Supreme Self.It is recommended in the Upanishads, that one should meditate on the Self, who is known to the mind, as the controller and ruler of all, taking the form of Prana, ether etc and is of true will. Though Brahman pervades the Universe, mode of meditation in one place, is different from the other. The mode of Purusha vidya [knowledge of self in the context of sacrifice], as also the fruits obtained thereof, varies from text to text. Those who meditate on Brahman can achieve their objects, even without deeds. The meditators who are engaged in various vidyas also attain Brahman. In the case of higher meditations all the attributes of the imperishable Brahman, like neither gross nor minute, invisible etc have to be included, because Brahman is apprenhended to be a single object.

The Supreme Lord, who has the heart as His abode, should be meditated with qualities of being free from evil, possessing true will and the ruler of all. The scriptures say that Brahman is not of material nature. As meditation on Udgitha gives powerful effect to the sacrifice, meditation on Udgitha is recommended in all sacrifices. There will be repetition of meditation on Brahman, when He is viewed to possess various qualities, one after another. Various objects of meditation with the words "Sambhu", "Shiva", etc specify that these objects are nothing but Narayana [Supreme Brahman]. Meditation is focusing the mind on Brahman. Whatever fruit is obtained by fire sacrifices, can be obtained through meditation. In meditating the highest as the self, one should realise His state of virtues comprising freedom from evil etc, which virtues manifest themselves, when he is released from the bondage of Samsara. In order to have unlimited enjoyment, Brahman alone should be meditated in the aggregate form, as the fruit thereof is His attainment alone. The modes of meditation other than Brahman, grant only limited fruits. The illustrious Badarayana thinks that the ultimate benefit of life results from vidya, as the knower of Brahman reaches the highest. A person who has learnt the vedas from the house of teachers, must lead a family life, upon coming back. This shows that works must be performed by him who has learnt the vedas. The scriptural texts show the destruction of works [good and bad], throughvidya, when the highest is beheld. Similarly persons who live a life of perpetual celibacy possessvidya, even though they do not perform fire sacrifices. Hencevidya cannot form an integral part of works. Sage Badarayana is of the opinion, that other stages of life [Brahmacharin or life before that of house holder, life in the forest or

Vanaprastha and Sannyasin or a renouncer], should be accomplished in the same way as the life of house holder. The passages narrating the stories are intended to establish injunctions in regard to vidya. A house holder must be calm and keep the senses under control, while performing works. All evil works that stand in the way of the rise of vidya, should be removed. The life of an Asramin or a person in various stages of life [Brahmacharin, Householder, Vanaprastha, Sannyasin] is better than that of him, who is not so. However, a Naisthika or perfect Brahmacharin must practice vow of celibacy, till his death. There are no expiatory ceremonies for transgressing the rules of Naisthika and such persons are excluded from performing religious works. Vidya belongs to the members of all Asramas. The fruits of meditation is obtained after clearing the obstacles, that stand in the way. When mind etc. are meditated, they have to be considered as forms of Brahman, as Brahman is superior to mind. Meditation on Brahman [to be done till death] destroys all kinds of sins. Some good and bad deeds begin to yield fruits. These fruits have to be enjoyed in one or many lives. Having destroyed the two kinds of deeds by enjoyment of their fruits, he reaches Brahman. The qualities of the individual self, similar to Brahman like unlimited knowledge and freedom from evil, manifests itself on reaching Brahman, when he is freed from the bondage of Karma. The released soul, in the absence of the body, experiences pleasure etc with the instruments created by the Supreme Self, as in the state of dream. When he has a body, he enjoys the pleasures as in the state of waking. Thus, the liberated self experiences unsurpassed bliss and does not return to this world again.

END NOTES

1. 10 senses consists of five organs of knowledge namely ear, skin, eye, tongue and nose and five organs of action namely speech, hands, feet, evacuation and generative organa.

CHAPTER - 3

VEDARTHA SANGRAHA

The individual souls attain heavenly, human, animal and plant bodies, due to accumulation of beginningless karma, brought about by ignorance, as it associates with matter, though it has knowledge and bliss, as its attributes.

From this it follows, that the same individual can be associated with actions, in past and the present. However, an individual who worships the Supreme Person, after understanding Him, attains the Brahman, which is of the nature of infinite bliss, when the effects of karma are destroyed. The Supreme Being is the material and instrumental cause of sentient and non-sentient beings, besides being its controller [[1]ref article on Vedanta Sara]. From this, it is clear that the individual soul can have names, only by virtue of Brahman, being its indwelling soul.

Brahman has as the instruments of His mighty sport and forming His own parts, an infinite number of individual souls, bound as well as free and also the physical universe. The latter has the power of passing through evolutions, where various living beings emerge from earlier forms, marvelous and boundless. Karma in the form of nescience, brings about the contraction of consciousness, that is an eternal attribute of the Atman or self. By virtue of this contraction, arises the wrong attitude to the self, and takes the bodies of Gods, men or any other creature, experiencing pleasures and pain. Thus, it is subject to persistent afflictions of Samsara. It has been maintained that this nescience, veils the nature of Brahman. The theme of scriptures comprehends principles, not determinable by perception. They are the nature of Brahman, characterised by infinite attributes like omniscience, pervading in all as their ultimate Self and absolute reality. Attainment of Brahman follows various modes of worship like sincere meditation.

The following conclusion is arrived from the various theories of Upanishads and Gita:-

Brahman consisting of all the sentient and non-sentient beings, is the ultimate. Brahman having the characteristics of changelessness and free from flaws exist in Prakriti and Jivatman as the indwelling self.

Vishnu's abode or Paramapada is beyond objects, characterized by the three qualities of Sattva, Rajas and Tamas. While Brahman is devoid of evil characteristics of Prakriti with its three-fold properties of Sattva, Rajas and Tamas, individual souls are caught up in Prakriti, due to nescience. The Supreme Lord, known as Narayana, who has the splendor of one lakh suns, bears eternally the conch, discus, mace, sword, bow and vanamala [garland of forest flowers] with Srivatsa mark on His chest, and also Goddess Lakshmi. Even as He is all pervading, the Goddess is also all pervading.

Prakriti [primordial matter] and Purusha [sum total of individual selves] constitute the body of the Supreme. Persons chosen by the Supreme Person attain Brahman, through devotion or Bhakti [experiencing joy in the Supreme], after understanding the nature of reality through scriptures. The individual self, which is different from the body is of the nature of consciousness and is subsidiary to the Supreme. Dependence on anyone other than the Supreme Person, is painful, as they are unworthy of service.

The soul is the controller of the body. The senses, including the mind of all beings [like Gods and men], do not comprehend Brahman, who is the inner ruler and very soul of all beings like Gods and men. As Brahman pervades the individual selves, He is subtler than the individual selves. Meditation is the instrument for attaining Him. Gita says that wise men can know the essential nature of the Self [Brahman], even though they are associated with various kinds of bodies. The texts maintain that Brahman is distinct from all and all else is subordinate to Him, while He is their Supreme Ruler. Modification in the nature of Brahman is denied. The direct means for achievement of immortality is to understand the difference between the individual self and the Supreme Controller. The Supreme Being endows all sentient beings with the power of thought and power of action. If an individual by himself is engaged in pursuit of what is most in accordance with the will of God, God is pleased with him. If on the other hand, an individual is pursuing what is most contrary to the divine will, the Lord gives him evil intellect and motivates him to proceed along evil lines. By controlling the mind and senses, an aspirant for Mukti [liberation], who has acquired knowledge from the scriptures, develops forgiveness, non-violence and offers obeisance to the Supreme Lord. Bhakti develops in such a devotee and through such Bhakti, the Supreme is attained. Those who have Sattva for quality, have a taste for vedas, which originates knowledge and enable him to reach the highest goal. In the texts having Tamas for its quality, Agni and Shiva are praised and in the texts having Rajas for its quality, Brahma is praised and in texts having Sattva for its quality, Hari is praised. Even the four-faced Brahma is subject to bondage. Those who know Narayana by His grace, as stainless become immortal and others sink in sorrow. It is impossible to imagine any other being, either equal or superior to Lord Narayana. The root of all vedas is said to be Pranav [AUM] and the letter "A" signifies the Supreme Lord. The Supreme Lord Narayana exists as the inner Self of Rudra, Brahma and all other embodied beings. This is as per vedas. Lord Narayana is greater than the greatest. As per Sri Vishnu Purana, Supreme Brahman is eternal, unborn, imperishable and undecaying. Four-faced Brahma and other individual selves, being subject to karma, are compelled to take birth in physical bodies. Lord Narayana, out of his own desire, in His supremely holy form, takes many births among Gods, men etc., for the purpose of effecting the good of the world. All texts of Upanishads impart knowledge of Brahman. Vedantic texts inculcate action in the form of meditation. Bhagwan Yamunacharya states that one attains immortality through vidya and performing duties pertaining to one's station in life. All entities, sentient and non-sentient, eternal and non-eternal, have as their sole nature, the character of being valued through a desire to make some special contribution to the Supreme [they are called Shesha]. The other is the sheshin [that to which the subsidiary contributes something special]. This is the case of servant's nature, being valued on account of the desire to contribute something special to the master. Those who understand the vedas, maintain that the Supreme Lord, being worshipped through various religious performances, rewards the worshippers with the objects they desire. The Supreme Soul accepts all performances, enjoined by the vedas and smrutis, ordinarily thought of as associated with deities like Indra and Agni, as He dwells in all deities as their inner soul. Even as the Supreme Person is eternal, the system of words embodying the knowledge concerning Him, His worship and the fruits accruing therefrom is eternal. Thus, in all vedas, Ithihasas and Puranas, we learn that all religious acts are of the nature of worship of Supreme Lord. He, the Supreme Person, so worshipped through them, grants all the desired fruits upto the very attainment of Him, as well as freedom from fear. Those who do not meditate on Him and indulge in actions prohibited, will through His disfavour, have as their lot measureless sorrow and fear, due to non-attainment of Him.

CHAPTER - 4

SRI BHASHYA

SRI BHASHYA - 1

Sri Ramanuja begins the Sri Bhashya with a prayer to Lord Narayana along with His consort, Goddess Lakshmi. After acquiring the knowledge of the vedic sacrificial rites, one has to acquire the knowledge of the Brahman, as it gives rise to liberation from Samsara [worldly existence] while works [sacrificial rites] result in the attainment of Swarga [heaven] and other similar things, which is destructible.

Study of vedas helps us to acquire the knowledge of Brahman. Hearing, reflecting over and over again and steady meditation on Brahman, removes ignorance or Avidya.

As per the Advaita philosophy of Sri Shankara, Brahman, who is without form and attributes, alone is real and the world, which is based on distinctions like Gods, men, animals etc is unreal [caused by Maya or illusion] and once the ignorance [distinctions] are removed by knowledge, Brahman is perceived, which also results in destruction of bondage.

Use of works [all the works pertaining to their respective Asramas or various stages of life, have to be practised as long as the life lasts] like sacrifices etc. helps in increasing Sattva quality [quality of goodness], which results from destruction of Rajas and Tamas qualities [qualities of passion and ignorance].

As per Advaitin philosophy, false perception can be removed by knowledge, which is similar to the case of a rope being perceived as a serpent. However it is made out that it is not mere knowledge, which removes ignorance and attain liberation but devotion, meditation and worship. [Ritualistic elements like the Udgitha or Pranava OM are helpful in meditation]. Thus, steady meditation leads us to direct perception of Brahman. It is then made out that Brahman is not reached either by reflection, steady meditation or hearing the scriptures, but whomsoever is chosen by

Him alone, is He reached. The word worship is the same as Bhakti [devotion]. Knowledge of Brahman is perceived by one whose mind is tranquilled and senses restrained. Past karmas [in the form of merit and demerit] result in the obstructiveness to the origination of knowledge of Brahman. Its destruction results from works performed, without attachment to results.

As per the Advaitin standpoint Brahman is free from all attributes. Perception of various distinctions like God, men etc., is due to beginningless Avidya or ignorance caused by Maya. However it is established that the things in this world are real as is the Brahman. It is further argued that since consciousness has its origin and liable to be destroyed, it cannot be the same as the individual self. In conditions of intoxication, swoons etc., where there is absence of absolute consciousness, egoism continues to persist. Next the quality of self is taken up for discussion. It is held that the self is the knower [awareness] and the knowership of the self does not contradict its immodifiable nature. Further self is different from body, senses, mind and vitality.

Experience is intelligible to the self [i.e. It consists of proving the existence of objects]. Intelligence [thinking logically] is present in all beings. By experience one can realise a thing. Consciousness exists due to its association with the self. [i.e. the luminosity is due to its association with the self]. The self denoted by "I" is the knower [ego of the self] and the knower is not subject to modifications.

Moreover the thing “I” is self-luminous like light and thus possesses the character of intelligence.The thing “I” is fully manifest in the waking state. However, though overpowered by darkness, it exists even during deep sleep. [During deep sleep the self exists as a witness of ignorance]. Even during final release the thing “I” continues to persist.

As self is eternal, so is its attribute, intelligence, eternal. The knowledge of the embodied individual self exists in a contracted condition due to its past actions [karmas]. The expansion and contraction of the self’s knowledge is by way of intelligence, which in turn is through the senses. Thus, the self acts as an agent due to its past karmas, though by nature it is immodifiable i.e. it is untouched by Prakriti, as well as qualities like sorrow, ignorance and greed, when it is free from karma. The self has no origination.

Avidya or ignorance, the cause of distinctions like Gods, men etc., due to Maya as per Advaitins is unoriginated having numerous modifications. Further they [Advaitins] believe that it is put to an end after origination of true knowledge [as per Advaitin philosophy].

Ahankara [material principle of egoity], otherwise called as pride, is non-intelligent and hence cannot possess the quality of knowership.

Just as the dreams, the cause of attainment of good and evil, are realistic, so are the scriptures, which forms the means for the attainment of Brahman. By knowing Brahman, who is omniscient, omnipotent, willing the truth, pervading as well as controlling all, who is denoted by Sat or existence, all things become known. The Advaitin viewpoint that Brahman is without attributes is contradicted, as Brahman has the qualities of Existence, knowledge and infinity not bound by time and space [Satyam, Jnanam and Anantam]. Further scriptural texts show that Brahman, the greatest Lord, who is free from sin, old age, death, sorrow, hunger, thirst etc, has the nature of intelligence and hence He is the knower.

Upanishads speak of the wind blowing due to the fear of the Brahman and also His unsurpassable bliss. Upanishads speak of Brahman existing in the small space inside the heart [Daharavidya] and by whose knowing, one attains the highest stage of liberation. Thus, the scriptural texts say that knowledge which is of the nature of worship, relating to Brahman, who is the soul of all beings leads to final release. The study of Upanishads, spoken of as the head of vedas or Vedanta, through a preceptor, helps in removing ignorance and attain the knowledge of the self along with Brahman. Brahman, who is the instrumental and material cause of the Universe, is established as being free from evil, possessing all auspicious qualities and is engaged in the creation, preservation and destruction of the world, for His mere sport. The world, consisting of intelligent and non-intelligent things, which constitutes the body of Brahman, is as real as Brahman. [All non-intelligent things like matter constitute the object of enjoyment, the intelligent thing i.e. the self are the enjoyers thereof and Brahman is the supreme ruler]. Due to ignorance [Avidya], the self is engaged in acts [meritorious as well as sinful] and hence does not remember that he is intelligent. Yoga [meditating on Vishnu] is stated to be the only remedy to bring about the cessation of circuit of mundane existence.

The Ithihasas and puranas explain the meaning of the vedas in a clear manner. The soul in all bodies is the same. [dog, God, mean persons etc.]. The individual self and the Supreme soul are different just as body and the soul. The released soul [after giving up merits and sin] is equal to the Brahman except in the matter of creation and has movement in all the worlds.

Brahman [Vishnu] alone is the object of worship in all the vidyas relating to the Supreme being. Further Brahman does not exist where there is Avidya [or ignorance] as He is pure intelligence.

The advaitin viewpoint is that avidya or ignorance, is due to one's karma and having the nature of positive entity, as it is associated with "I".

In the case of dreams, as per the acts of a person [merit and sin], God himself creates the corresponding objects, capable of being perceived by particular persons and comes to an end after a particular length of time. As already stated, things in this world are as real as is the Brahman. The effect is nothing but the cause [modified]. The pleasures, pains etc are according to the merit and demerit of individual souls in the world created by Brahman. The Lord, who is the owner of Maya [Prakriti] creates the world wherein the individual self is bound down by Maya, due to Avidya. Prakriti, with its qualities of goodness or Sattva, passion or Rajas and ignorance or Tamas, is called as Maya as it creates wonderful things and is associated with Avidya..

Hence Avidya cannot be described as an entity or non-entity as per Advaitins.

Self is of the nature of intelligence, is unoriginated and eternal and hence termed existence. But the non-intelligent part, also termed as Prakriti [e.g.: human body, God, mountains, rivers etc], which forms the object of enjoyment for the individual selves is subject to destruction and modification as per the Karma [action] of the individual selves and is therefore termed non-existence and unreal. Both the existent and non-existent things forms the body of Mahavishnu, the Self of the world and the Supreme ruler, both in the gross and subtle states [Pralaya]. When freed from Karma [merits and demerits], the self manifests in its own form.

The Advaitin viewpoint that Brahman is without attributes and ignorance [owing to meritorious and unmeritorious karmas], the cause of self possessing bodies like God, men etc., is ceased by means of knowledge is contradicted and it is held that final release results from the divine worship of the Brahman, who is with attributes.

The material embodiments like men, God etc. is dependent on individual self for its existence. The self, unseen, enjoys the fruits of its karma, through the body.

Similarly the individual selves and the respective bodies like God, men etc. form the body of Brahman, who has intelligence as His attribute and is self-luminous.

The results of the sacrifices etc. by way of worship of other Gods is from the Supreme Brahman alone.

The omnipotent and omniscient Brahman, who wills the truth is the cause of creation, preservation and destruction of the world. The only means of proving Brahman, whose essential nature is different from all other things, is the scriptures [shastras].

Brahman creates the world by His mere will.

The Advaitin's contention that Brahman cannot be known by Shastras or meditation but only on the dawn of knowledge is contended. The Advaitins also argue that final release follows immediately after the dawn of knowledge. [when perception of distinctions like God, men etc., caused by Maya is removed]. Finally it is established that Brahman, who has innumerable auspicious qualities devoid of slightest taint of evil, is really existent and the cause of the world, with the objective of the Vedanta being meditation [worship], when non-distinction becomes a reality and bondage comes to an end.

This is similar to the case of a lost son [bonded individual self], who on realisation that his father is the king and alive [on realisation of Brahman], becomes extremely happy. Likewise the king [Brahman] is happy to receive his son [bonded individual self] back, hale and healthy.

Brahman is different from the individual self, as even the released self [who possesses the auspicious qualities of Brahman] does not have the power to create worlds. The bound individual self, due to beginningless karma, is different from the Brahman, as well as other individual selves. The evils of the individual self does not accrue to the Brahman.

Pradhana [primordial matter] cannot be the cause of the world because it is not possible for non-intelligent Pradhana to be involved in the activities of seeing and thinking, which forms the basis for creation, as per the scriptures.

Morever the world consisting of intelligent and non-intelligent things has Brahman for its Self. Final release [or salvation] is not obtained to those who worship Pradhana. If Pradhana was to be the cause of the world, by knowing Pradhana, the totality of intelligent and non-intelligent things should have been known. However by knowing Pradhana all intelligent and non-intelligent things cannot be known. Morever the Upanishads speak of the union of the individual self with the Brahman, during times of deep sleep.

Brahman is the cause of the worlds, as the five elements [ether, air, fire, water and earth] originated from Him as per the Upanishads. The Upanishads also speak of the intelligent Brahman, the Self of all, with qualities of omniscience and free from evil, being the cause of the world, with differentiation in names and forms in the gross state.

The Advaitin viewpoint that Brahman is devoid of attributes is contended as Brahman is an intelligent being unlike Pradhana.

Anandamaya or the highest bliss is the Brahman and the individual self when freed from matter, has the final object of attainment of Brahman, who is existence, knowledge and infinity. Thus Brahman is different from all things including pain.

The individual self is capable of enjoying only a small amount of pleasure mixed with endless miseries. The world has the Brahman for its Self. Brahman created the whole world consisting of the five gross elements etc., giving bodies to God, men etc., with individual selves entering those bodies as per their karma and Himself entered into the individual selves to form their Self. Thus, Brahman is associated with non-intelligent matter and the intelligent individual self in the gross state, where there is differentiation in names and forms. The evils of the individual self do not taint the Brahman, whose body is the Universe, as childhood, youth etc. do not affect the individual self. Thus, the Anandamaya or the highest bliss is different from the individual self, who is having knowledge or understanding as the attribute. The Ananda or the highest bliss is the Brahman because the bliss succeeding the individual self is hundred fold of the bliss preceding it. However, there can be no modification of the bliss in relation to the supreme self. Further Brahman is devoid of misery even to a small extent as the Upanishads state that He is devoid of sin. Further the cause of bliss to the individual selves is the highest Self. Hence the highest bliss is the Supreme Self. Further the object to be attained by the individual self, who is the worshipper, is the Supreme Self. Further one who knows the bliss of the Brahman will not be born again in this world. Brahman, the creator of ether etc. is not the individual self. Further Brahman, without associating with Pradhana, created the worlds by mere will, unlike the individual self, who is associated with Pradhana. Hence the highest bliss is the Brahman, different from the individual self. The scriptures also declare the individual self acquiring the bliss due to Brahman.

He, who is within the sun and the eye is the Brahman because He is spoken of as devoid of sin [i.e. free from karma] with His attributes being the Lordship of the worlds, desires etc., possessing a body out of His own will and not due to karma [different from the bodies got by karma], for the protection of the good. egs: Lord Rama, Krishna etc., Further He is the ruler of individual selves like sun etc. but those selves do not know Him as their ruler.

Brahman [Narayana] is denoted by Akasa [ether] as He is the cause as well as the dissolution of the world, consisting of intelligent and non-intelligent things.

Similarly Brahman is denoted by "Prana", as all animate and inanimate things [like stone etc.] are created by Him.

The word "Jyotis" is the Brahman, because His one feet make up the living beings while His three immortal feet are in the highest heaven.

The word "Gayatri" also denotes the Brahman, as He is the self of all beings, with one foot making the living beings and three immortal feet in Highest heaven, as per the scriptures.

Similarly the words "Indra" and "Prana" denote the Brahman because He forms the support of intelligent and non intelligent things, besides having qualities of bliss, non-decay, Immortality, forming the Self of all, whose worship is three-fold. [continued meditation on the Brahman being the cause of the worlds, having the enjoyers [individual selves] as well as the enjoyable [material things] for His body].

SRI BHASHYA - 2

As per the scriptures, omniscient and omnipotent Brahman, the Self of all individual selves as well as matter, who is devoid of sin and is the cause of creation, sustenance and destruction of the world, is the object of worship.

Though the released self is identical with Brahman, he does not undertake works like creation etc. of this world. Brahman, who is the supporter of all living beings is apprehended only by mind, which is purified by worship.

Though the Supreme Self resides in the heart, He is greater than all the worlds [Chandogya Upanishad]. However, He is not subject to pleasures and pain, as He is free from karma and sins.

It is mentioned in the Kathopanishad that the eater of Brahmanas and Kshatriyas is the Supreme Self, implying that all movable and immovable things are absorbed in Brahman, at the time of deluge [pralaya]. However, Brahman remains distinct from matter [immovable things] and the individual selves [movable things] during the state of dissolution.

The individual soul [born of Brahman] attains liberation [Moksha], on removal of ignorance [as the fruit of worship], brought about by beginning-less karma, when the Supreme Self is realised. Upakosala is taught by the fires that Brahman is life, supreme happiness and the ether of space.

The person who is seen within the eye is the Brahman, as He is spoken of as being immortal, fearless and having supreme happiness as his attribute. A person who experiences Brahman sees nothing other Him, because the totality of all things is included in Brahman. Further nothing other than Him was in existence in the subtle state. [Chandogya Upanishad]. Further the person who is within the eye is spoken as the light which leads to final release.

Similarly the words ether [or Akasa] and Prana [principal vital air] denotes Brahman, as ether mentioned here has the quality of supreme happiness and Prana mentioned here, is the support of the whole world. The invisible being denoted by Akshara is the Supreme being because of his attributes of omniscience, being the source of creation, having Universal form and by whose knowing, all things become known. The term "Vaisvanara" denotes the Supreme self and not the gastric fire as this Vaisvanara has an Universal form, having the three worlds for His body and is worshipped by kings like Asvapati for attaining final release.The term "Bhuman" [meaning great one] denotes Brahman because He is synonymous with truth, having the nature of bliss, and is different from individual soul denoted by the word "Prana". The term "Akshara" means the Supreme Brahman because it is described as the support of Prakriti or Pradhana and which is beyond Akasa or sky and forms the source of Prakriti or Pradhana. Further knowledge of Akshara leads a person to Brahman while ignorance of it leads to worldly life. The term "Akasa" denotes the Supreme being and not the individual self, as the individual self does not perform acts relating to the creation of worlds and as the individual self rests in Brahman in conditions of deep sleep Brahman who is free from sins, without undergoing modifications, is the internal ruler, controlling the deities presiding over the great elements, celestial objects as well as the internal self and the senses, existing as well as having a body, in each of them and unknown to them.Though Brahman is immeasurable, He is associated with a material body, for the purpose of worship. However, a person with loving devotion and knowledge of scriptures, must be the one chosen by Brahman for attaining Brahman.

He who abides in the heaven, earth etc. is the Supreme being because He is spoken of as the bridge leading to immortality, pervading all things and is the object of attainment to those who have given up merit and demerit, without association with Prakriti.The little ether in the lotus-like heart is the Supreme Brahman [denoted by dahara-akasa], as He is devoid of sin, old age, death, sorrow, hunger and wills the truth. Moreover the dahara-akasa is spoken as the abode as well as the support of all the worlds. Hence dahara-akasa denotes the Brahman, who is the object of worship.

The individual self, who is ridden with misery cannot be the one residing in heaven, earth etc.

The world consists of pain when it is distinct from Brahman. However, the same world becomes bliss experiencing Brahman [the Self of all including the individual self and is the cause of creation], when it is freed from karma.

He who utters the syllable "OM" [three mantras] attains Brahman, who is free from fear, old age and death.

Individual self takes birth in various bodies till he is liberated, on account of sins.

Moreover the individual self is not aware [owing to ignorance] of the Brahman [mentioned as dahara-akasa], even though he moves in that direction everyday [during deep sleep]. The individual self, whose ignorance is removed by worship etc., attains bliss on reaching Brahman. However, the individual self is different from Brahman, as he is incapable of undergoing activities like creation.

He, who is of the size of thumb [located in the interior of heart] is the Brahman, for He is spoken of as the Lord of the past, present and the future. [As the heart of humans is of the size of thumb and as Brahman resides in heart region, humans alone in this world are qualified to worship the Brahman]. However, Gods who possess bodies are also qualified to worship the Brahman as they too are bound by karma.

Gods like Indra propitiated in sacrifices may take many bodies as in the case of Rishi Saubhari. [Gods like Indra refer to a class as after one Indra, another Indra takes over].

That the Vedas are eternal is substantiated by the fact that creation continues even after dissolution because of continuous identity in names and forms of all beings.

Brahman created the worlds by teaching the vedas to four- faced Brahma [Hiranyagarbha], while residing inside Hiranyagarbha as the internal self. [The Highest person bears the vedas in mind in a proper order]. Brahman first created water and the four-faced Brahma emerged from the lotus, from where the worlds consisting of Gods, men etc were created. [As the current Brahma is in his 51st year, creation has taken place 50*360 times, by the current Brahma, with creation taking place, during the day of Brahma].

Although persons belonging to the Fourth varna [varna is division of society on the basis of occupation in ancient India], are not entitled to study the vedas, still they may eradicate their sins by studying Ithihasas and puranas.

The wind blows and the sun shines due to the fear of the person who is of the size of thumb and is the internal Self of all beings. [Brahman]. The highest Self [Lord] is celebrated under the name of Vishnu, in the Vedas and Vedanta, as per Sri Vishnu Purana.

The Supreme Self is the supporter and ruler of all the worlds, the characteristics of which cannot belong to the individual self, even in the state of liberation.

It is held that the body is superior to the individual self, as the individual self is dependant on the body for its activities. However, the Supreme Self, the internal self of all beings, is superior to the body, as all activities depend on His will and is the goal of attainment. [can be attained by bringing the senses under control].

Prakriti[1] or primordial matter which is spoken as "Aja" produces numerous offspring having the qualities of Sattva, Tamas and Rajas [white, black and red in colour], having Brahman for its self. The Lord creates the Maya [Prakriti] for the enjoyment of the individual self, as the individual self is bound by Maya.

Yama also spoke to Nachiketas about the God, who resides in the cave of the heart and is the inner controller of all beings, by whose knowing through worship, the soul having given up pleasures and pain, attains immortality.

It is also mentioned that the unborn female being [Aja or Prakriti] is enjoyed by one being under the influence of karma and given up by the other being [freed soul] after enjoying her. [when sins are destroyed by worshipping Brahman]. Moreover it is mentioned that "Aja" has light for its source [the cause of Prakriti is Brahman] and hence not independent. The "Aja" [Prakriti] exists in subtle form at the time of universal dissolution [& hence unborn], without differentiation of names and forms and in condition of effect exists with differentiation of names and forms [after creation takes place].

The Sankhya's contention that one who knows the individual self, consisting of 25 principles [Groups of five] and ether[2] becomes immortal is refuted by Sri Ramanuja, who says that by knowing Brahman, the controller of the five senses and mind, one becomes immortal.

It is evident that the omniscient Brahman is the cause of the worlds, as He entered the worlds, for the purpose of controlling it, after creating it, which is not possible for non-intelligent Pradhana. Pradhana's existence and non-existence is during its evolved and unevolved conditions.

The Sankhyas, citing Kaushitaki Upanishad argue that creation is brought about by the individual self [who presides over the Pradhana], by virtue of its association with karma. The individual selves become objects of enjoyment to one another through their karma and creation takes place to undergo the karma. In conditions of deep sleep, when there is no dreaming, speech and the senses rest in the individual self. [referred to as prana]. However, Sri Ramanuja says that the prana referred to here is the Brahman. Thus, the individual self enjoys all things created by Brahman, who is different from the individual self and principal vital air, in accordance with its karma.

The husband becomes dear to the wife in accordance with the wishes of Brahman [Self] and hence one has to become dear to the Supreme being, for attaining immortality and not with the husband, wife, son, wealth etc. who are associated with pleasures and pain and whose wishes depend on the Supreme being. Morever it is only by knowing the Supreme being, knowledge of all animate and inanimate objects becomes known. [All things existed in the Supreme Self before creation]. Final freedom arises by worshipping Supreme Brahman, the cause of the world, who abides as the Self of the individual self.

Thus, the teachings of Kapila, which states that Pradhana and four-faced Brahma, not having Brahman for its self, is the material cause of the world, is rejected.

Brahman, the Self of animate and inanimate objects and who is distinct from everything [being free from old age, death, sorrow, hunger, thirst and karma] is established to be both the material and instrumental cause of the world, as by knowing Brahman, the whole world becomes known. [In the case of pots, clay is the material cause, potter the instrumental cause and pot is the effect- Pot, the effect is nothing but the cause i.e. clay, modified]. Thus, Brahman, who is omniscient and omnipotent, possessing unlimited knowledge and bliss, without any evil, binds the individual self by His Maya [illusion].

Brahman is the cause of origin of non-intelligent things like earth, rivers, oceans, mountains etc. and the puranas maintain that they too have consciousness.

Non-intelligent things like water, having consciousness is because of the dieties controlling them.

Brahman, who is without slightest taint of evil is the cause of intelligent and non-intelligent things of the world.

As the soul does not undergo changes like the body [childhood, youth, old age etc.] and the body is not associated with knowledge, happiness etc., which is associated with the soul, so also Brahman, whose essential nature does not change, though present in the heart region, is devoid of pleasures and pain, as He is devoid of karma. Pleasures and pain, which is due to ignorance, are experienced by individual souls due to their past karma, while Brahman does not experience the same, as He is free from karma, both in subtle and gross conditions. Thus we find Brahman, to be different from the individual self as well as inanimate objects like stone etc. as He is distinct from all things other than Himself, having all powers and devoid of sin, having a mine of auspicious qualities. However, the Lord, though without karma, out of his own free will, takes various incarnations, unlike the individual souls, who are born as per their karma.

According to Advaitin's philosophy, Brahman, the cause alone is real, while the world we perceive, being the effect is unreal. Giving an example, they say that the pot [effect] is unreal, while clay [cause] alone is real. However, Swetaketu is taught by his father, that the pots are as real as is the clay.

Thus, the world is as real as is the Brahman. [During Pralaya or Universal dissolution, His body consists of intelligent [Purusha] and non-intelligent things [Prakriti] in subtle condition, while in gross condition [during creation] they are differentiated by names and forms. Thus, by knowing Brahman, the whole world which is the effect, becomes known. Further the Advaitin's view that a single soul constitute all bodies is refuted, as the experience of each soul is different. In the case of Saubhari, by means of one self, the recognition of pleasures etc arising out of many bodies, was seen in relation to one person. [For story of Rishi Saubhari ref Srimad Bhagavatham canto 9 chapter 6 verse 38-55]

Just as milk is converted to curds, Brahman, though indivisible and unchangeable, by His mere will, creates the Universe for His sport. Partiality in creation does not arise as creation is based on one's karma [acts]. Further karma and selves are beginingless.

The self is indeed the knower and the material principle of egoity, is not the knower, as it is non-intelligent. The Supreme Brahman is distinct from the individual self as per Brihadaranyaka Upanishad. Brahman is capable of producing effect, as He is distinct from all other things and associated with all the powers.

END NOTES

1. Prakriti, which is non-intelligent is produced by the intelligent Brahman, like scorpions produced from cowdung, meaning different dung types support different insect communities [Ref: Peter Skidmore's book on "Insects of the cowdung community" where Reaumur has stated that different dung types support different insect communities".
2. 5 each of gross and subtle elements, 5 each of organs of knowledge and action, Mahat [intelligence], Prakriti [primordial matter], Purusa [soul], mind, Ahankara [ego] and ether [mentioned again because of its importance and distinctive quality]

SRI BHASHYA - 3

The Sankhya philosophy is that Pradhana 25 in number, with its qualities of goodness, passion and ignorance in conditions of equilibrium during Pralaya or dissolution and subject to modifications, is the cause of the world. However, it is held that Pradhana, which is unintelligent, without being presided by an intelligent being [Brahman], is incapable of producing things, just as wood cannot be made chariots, unless presided by one, who knows how to make them. Hence Pradhana [which is non-existent during dissolution], with its qualities of goodness, passion and ignorance cannot undergo transformations, without being presided by Brahman. Further in the absence of knowership, Pradhana cannot be the cause of the world. Moreover due to proximity of the immodifiable and pure Purusha [self] with Prakriti, liberation will not be attained. The Sankhya's view that Pradhana is the cause of bondage as well as final release is inconsistent, as also the view of the Advaitin's, who do not accept that there are innumerable Purushas. [The Advaitin's also believe that Brahman is the witness of actions, which is inconsistent, as the self is the witness of actions].

Brahman, for His mere sport, creates the world. Inequalities in creation is due to past karma [the pleasures and pains are ascribed to Brahman's favour or disfavour]. Brahman also enters the individual selves for the purpose of controlling them. Brahman rewards those who act as per shastras and punishes those who act against the shastras. However, the Lord rewards His worshippers [by giving the power to worship Him], and also destroys their sins.

The Atomic theory is rejected as infinitesimal atoms, which have no extension in space, cannot unite to form the world. Secondly, the karmas of the individual selves are not found in non-intelligent atom. If it is admitted that the motion in atoms is due to the presence of the self, then creation has to be eternal, as karmas present in the self are eternal. [even during Pralaya or Universal dissolution]. Further atoms without the qualities of colour, taste, smell etc. cannot be the cause of fire, water, earth and air.

The momentary theory of Buddhists is rejected as a thing gets destroyed every moment. Thus, a thing produced subsequently will be from nothingness.

The Jaina's theory of existence and non-existence in the same thing cannot be accepted. Their view that the self has the dimensions of the body also cannot be accepted as the self of an elephant cannot pass into the body of an ant.

The doctrine that accepts Pasupati as the Supreme Lord is rejected as the Vedas assign that position to Narayana. The Pancharatra system is authoritative as it negatives the origination of the jiva or the self. The Supreme Lord takes various forms like Sankarshana, Pradyumna and Aniruddha, presiding over the self, mind and Ahankara [ego].

Brahman is the direct cause of spatial ether, air, fire, water and earth. Further the Upanishads say that the principal vital air [prana], mind and the senses are also created by Brahman, who is the self of all animate and inanimate things. [Brahman alone existed in the subtle state]. Further it is established that there are eleven senses [five organs of knowledge like ear, skin, eye, tongue and nose five organs of action like hands, feet, speech, excretory and genital organs and the mind]. Further the senses are atomic in size as they leave the body after death. Principal vital air [prana] is spoken as the form of air in a particular condition. The principal vital air is also an auxiliary instrument of the self like the eye, performing five-fold functions like Prana [main air passing through the nose], Apana [air passing through the rectum as evacuated bodily air], Vyana [total air circulating all over the body], Udana [air passing through the throat, stoppage of which constitutes suffocation] and Samana [air which adjusts the foodstuff in the stomach and which sometimes sounds as belching]. The principal vital air is also atomic in size.

The individual self has no origination as per the Upanishads. The Upanishads state that the individual self is the knower, having the attribute of intelligence, both in the bound and released states. However, there is expansion and contraction of knowledge, in the case of individual self. Further Jivatma is the eternal part of Brahman. [BG Chapter 15 verse 7]. In the case of Brahman, there is neither change of essential nature nor contraction and expansion of knowledge, as in the case of individual self. As the scriptures speak of the self moving out of the body and returning to it, the self is atomic in size. Though the individual self exists in the heart region, pleasures and pains are felt all over the body through the quality of knowledge. This is similar to the case of sandalpaste, whose effects are felt all over the body, though existing in a particular part of the body. The self has the attribute of intelligence all the time [even during deep sleep]. This is similar to masculinity manifesting in youth, though latent in boyhood. As the Upanishads state that the self seizes the sense organs and moves in the body as he pleases, the self is the agent as well as the enjoyer of actions, i.e. actions are performed only when desired by the self. However, the self performs actions with the consent of the Supreme being, who is present in the heart of all beings, as the internal ruler of all selves. [the control exercised over the senses by the individual self and the presiding dieties of the senses is as per the will of the Brahman]. The Lord, however, favours persons who do deeds as per shastras and disfavours persons who do wicked deeds as per shastras. Though the individual self is a part of Brahman as per vedic texts etc., they are different from one another and hence there is varied experience. Moreover the evils pertaining to the individual self does not attach the Brahman, just as luminosity of sun is different from the sun.

Permission and prohibition to study vedas etc. is based on the relationship with bodies.

After creating the egg-shaped Universe with the three components of earth, water and fire, the Supreme being created living beings [from the subtle state in Pralaya or universal dissolution to gross state].

While moving from one body to another, the individual self takes with it the sense organs and the material elements in a subtle state. At every stage, the five subtle elements undergo accordant transformations. On death, the presiding deities cease to preside over the respective senses.

Those who perform religious works ascend the heavenly world, on leaving the mortal body and after enjoying celestial pleasures, the self reaches the earth as rain after entering the clouds via space, air, smoke and subsequently gets associated with the plants, becoming the food and semen for the male and the semen so produced is thrown into the womb of woman, becoming the foetus in that woman [represented as a series of five oblations offered by sense organs]. As per the Upanishads, the individual self returns to this world from the path of Gods and manes [pitrus] with the balance of karmas.

Those who perform religious works go through the path of Gods and those who perform charitable deeds go through the path of manes and return to this world from moon. However, sinners, after undergoing sufferings in Hell, return to the world, to be born as germs, birds, reptiles etc. [without five oblations starting with association of ether, as in the case of humans]. While descending from moon, the self [the selves of all men where there are five oblations] has mere close contact with ether etc. Further the self does not stay there for long. There is no mention of karma to be born as paddy etc., as the body is obtained only after reaching the womb of woman.

The objects seen in dreams are created by the Supreme person as good dreams are indicative of auspiciousness and bad dreams indicate evil to follow. [prior to his departure to Ayodhya from Kekaya kingdom Bharata had ominous dreams portending the death of his father, Dasaratha [Valmiki

Ramayana, Ayodhyakanda]. During deep sleep, the self sleeps in the Brahman, who is in the pericardium, a membrane surrounding the heart. It is the same person who is in the state of dreamless sleep that rises on awakening. The case of swoon, where there is no consciousness, is considered a half-way state to death. The evils pertaining to the individual self in the states of dreaming, dreamless sleep and swoon does not accrue to the Supreme Brahman, as He is free from karma. Similarly the evils pertaining to the individual self of beings does not accrue to the Supreme Brahman, even though He is the Self of the individual self, as He is free from karma. The individual self possess form due to its association with past karmas. There is none higher than the Brahman, who is associated with the corporeal and incorporeal forms, which are His parts both in the subtle and gross states, in terms of qualities or essential nature. [Though the non-intelligent world as well as the individual self form parts of Brahman, they are distinct from Him, like sun and light]. Brahman can be known only by scriptures [as per the Vedas, He can be apprehended by worship or steady meditation]. Moreover Brahman is the means and the goal of attainment.

Though Brahman is immeasurable, His description of measure is meant only for worship. The various fruits like worldly prosperity, salvation etc. is by invoking Brahman, who is all pervasive, either directly or through other Gods, whose internal controller is the Brahman. The worship of Brahman in all Vedantic texts is the same [e.g.: Vaisvanara, Dahara etc] and the fruit is the attainment of Brahman. In regard to two identical meditations, the constituent elements of each have to be transferred to the other and combined with the latter's elements.

Meditation on Udgitha Vidya [syllable "OM"] with the view of prana or vital air leads to defeat of enemies. Ways of Meditation on the Udgitha, is spoken differently in different Upanishads. Further meditation on the Udgitha, which is present in all branches of the veda, in sacrifices is optional, as the fruits are different from those of the sacrificial rites. In the Taittiriya Upanishad, the Supreme self is denoted by the word "prana" as He is engaged in creation. Prana has to be clothed by sipping water before and after taking food, as per the Upanishads. Ushastha and Kahola, both disciples of Yajnavalka, are taught in the same vidya that Brahman is the internal self, sustaining life in all beings through prana [principal vital air] and who transcends hunger, thirst, sorrow, old age and death.

There is no particular form of meditation for attaining Brahman, as per Upanishads. The essential qualities of Brahman like existence, knowledge, bliss, purity and infinity are to be included in all vidyas. [meditation on Brahman]. In the course of meditation on Brahman, additional qualities like controller of all is to be included in the quality of willng the truth and hence the two meditations are identical. Meditations of Brahman residing in the orb of the sun and the eye are considered to be different. However, Brahman, with qualities of willing the truth and ruler of all, is considered to be the same vidya, as in both the cases He has the heart as the abode. Similarly Brahman pervading the heaven and supporting the eldest powers cannot be included in all meditations. If the qualities described in the two vidyas are different, they are considered to be distinct Vedic mantras or ritual are not auxiliary to vidya. For a man of vidya, giving up sin and merit is declared. [merits reaching friends and sins reaching enemies]. For meditators on Brahman, both the meritorious and sinful deeds are given up at the time of death and the soul travels through the path of Gods with a subtle body. However, for sages like Vasistha, destruction of meritorious and sinful deeds last till they hold the position of sage [does not take place upon death]. It is further established in the Upanishads that a person who meditates on the Brahman, with His auspicious qualities like desiring the truth, has free movement in all the worlds [i.e. on attaining liberation]. Meditation on the qualities of the Supreme Brahman has to be repeated. Lord Narayana [Supreme Brahman] is the object of worship in all meditations. The mental activities [chanting slokas, reading spiritual texts etc.] of a person per day, whose life span is taken as 100 years, is considered as a fire [sacrifice of knowledge] and hence there are 36000 fires, which is considered as distinct from the sacrifice of action [fire rituals etc]. The fruits obtained by the sacrifice of action, is the same as obtained by nature of meditation.The Supreme Self should be meditated as residing within the body of released individual self [self who has attained liberation]. The worship of the Supreme Brahman as Vaisvanara or Bhuman has to be made treating the bodies of Vaisvanara or Bhuman as a whole and not as parts. The vidyas concerning the auspicious qualities of Brahman are considered to be different. Cumulation of vidyas is not advised for vidyas concerning the fruit of Brahman, where supreme bliss is attained. However, where it does not concern the fruit of Brahman, cumulation of vidyas is recommended. [because if Brahman can be attained by one vidya, there is no use of other vidyas].

Brahman, who is free from all evil and hence different from the individual self is the object of meditation [meditating on Brahman is vidya] and this vidya is not accessory to karma, as Upanishads say that the householder can renounce householder's life [performing charity etc.] in order to attain Brahman. Further karmas [good and bad works] get destroyed on acquiring the knowledge of Brahman. Hence vidya is not accessory to karma. Similarly student, anchorite in the forest, wandering ascetic and householder who wish to renounce householder's life, in their quest for knowledge relating to Brahman do not perform karma [works]. Hence vidya, which is the highest object of human pursuit is not accessory to karma. As the duties of the Asramas are helpful in the production of vidya, they have to be performed as auxiliaries to vidya. Thus, even celibates are entitled to practise vidyas, which is seen to be the means of attainment of the highest object of human pursuit.

In Vedantic passages stories are told to make us understand the rules regarding vidya. Similarly stories in earlier part of vedas tell us about the rules regarding rituals. Rituals, giving gifts etc. are necessary for a householder practising vidya, while it is not necessary for celibates. Further a householder must exercise tranquility and self-restraint while practicing vidya. For a knower of Brahman, permission to eat all foods [left overs etc] is permitted when there is danger to life. Duties of the respective ashramas should not be given up, even if they do not desire vidya.

A widower and a bachelor, who has finished his studies are also entitled to vidya. However, perpetual celibates, anchorites and ascetics, who have fallen from their vows of celibacy are not entitled to vidya. The meditation on the Udgitha has to be performed by the sacrificer, with the priest as the agent. After attaining child-like qualities [not exhibiting one's greatness], one should worship the Brahman, thinking over the form of the Lord. A person who worships the Brahman attains salvation, irrespective of the ashram to which he is attached. [4 ashrams-student, householder, forest dweller and wandering ascetic]. Knowledge of vidya, either for worldly prosperity or for attaining salvation will produce immediate results, if there is no obstruction [committing offence against knowers of Brahman]. Meditation on the Brahman has to be practised repeatedly, A worshipper should worship the Brahman, as residing within his self. In the case of meditation, symbol [mind,conch,discus etc.] has to be viewed as Brahman, as Brahman is superior. Similarly Udgitha has to be viewed as the Sun-God, as Sun-God is superior. Meditation should be performed only when one is seated, where there is concentration. Further meditation should be performed till the end of life.

A person of vidya after destroying sins [committed before or after attainment of vidya- sins committed after attainment of vidya is through inadvertence] as well as meritorious deeds [committed before or after attainment of vidya] and which have not begun to yield fruits attain

Brahman. However, if the meritorious as well as sins have begun to yield fruits, Brahman is attained after exhausting them in one or more births [in case it is not possible to exhaust them in one birth].

Senses [semse of speech, touch, form, taste and smell] of the dying man rests in the mind, which in turn rests in the prana [principal vital air], which [prana] in turn rests in the individual self. The prana along with the individual self rests in the elements. The self's departure from the body is the same for one who knows vidya or not, upto the entry of blood vessels. However, for a man of vidya, the self departs from the 101st blood vessel present in the head Others [those without vidya] depart from other blood vessels. A man of vidya is connected with this world [samsara], till the attainment of Brahman, as subtle body which experiences heat follows him. [the first three hours of a dead body will be soft and warm]. The individual self along with the senses,Prana and the subtle elements rest for a moment in the Supreme Self, to seek relief from the agony of death. This association of the individual self in the Brahman is different from the association during Pralaya [universal dissolution]. As already stated the soul along with the subtle body of the man of vidya, lighted up by the Supreme Brahman passes through the 101st blood vessel in the head. The soul follows the rays of the sun as per the Upanishads. This applies for death which occur during nights, as heat is experienced even during nights. [the earth radiates heat into outer space during nights]. Similarly, a man of vidya, who dies during the southern course of the sun attains Brahman, after reaching moon.

A man of vidya is led to the Brahman through the dieties of light, day, bright fortnight, six months [northern course] and year [these are the escorting dieties], followed by Gods like Vayu, Varuna, Sun, Indra, Prajapati, superhuman being and the Brahman. It is mentioned that those who worship the Brahman as well as the individual selves,released from Prakriti, having Brahman for their selves, go along this path. The latter is like an inferior Mukti called Kaivalya, where there is bliss from self-realisation, but no experience of the Brahman in His fullness, as in the former case. After attaining Brahman and without being separated from Him, the individual self appears in its true nature. [ignorance being removed, there is expansion of knowledge and bliss which was contracted by karma and the individual self manifests in its true form, being free from sin etc.] Solely by his will, the released self gets everything that he wants [scriptural texts mention them as eating, playing and enjoying in the company of relatives etc.] The released self has only the Supreme Self as the ruler and none else. The released self can either have a body or remain without a body. The released self who has a body, can also have one or more bodies, as per his will, where his enjoyments will be that of a bound self in waking state. When he is without a body, his experiences will be like that of a bound self in dreams. [he will experience enjoyments with the help of a body created by the Supreme Self]. The released self is omniscient, the quality of which was absent in the bound state. However, the individual self is closely associated with the Lord, both in the bound and released states. The released self does not undertake works like Creation, sustenance and dissolution of the world. The released self enjoys eternal bliss by Lord's grace, in the worlds ruled by deities, who are manifestations of Brahman, with free movement in those worlds.

Further the released self will not fall into bondage again and return to this world.

CHAPTER - 5

SRI RAMANUJA'S GADYATRAYAM

1. SHARANAGATHI GADYAM OR TEXT OF SURRENDERING TO THE LORD

The text begins with salutations to Sri Ramanuja. Sri Ramanuja, next surrenders to the Supreme Lord, with a desire to offer selfless service always, through the divine mother Sridevi, who has qualities similar to the Lord. [The Goddess, who is merciful, pardons our sins and pleads with the Lord on our behalf].

After receiving Goddess Mahalakshmi's blessings, Sri Ramanuja describes the divine form of the Lord, which is full of brilliance. Then he describes the qualities of the Lord, which includes mercy, power, accessibility, affection, generosity and being free from flaws. Then he describes the divine ornaments which includes divine garlands, Srivathsa mole, Kaustubha jewel etc and divine weapons of the Lord like conch, discus, mace, sword, bow etc., which protect his devotees by destroying their foes. Sri Ramanuja then describes Sridevi, Bhudevi, and Neeladevi, possessing divine qualities as the consorts of the Lord. Permanent attendants of the Lord like Shesha, Garuda, Vishvaksena etc., who are endowed with noble qualities, act as per the wishes of the Lord.

Vaikunta or Paramapada is the land of eternal bliss with mansions, gardens, rivers etc meant for the enjoyment of the divine couple. Prakriti [nature], Jiva [individual self] and Time, assist the Lord in the sport of creation, sustenance and dissolution. Sri Ramanuja seeks refuge at the lotus feet of the Lord, renouncing father, mother, wealth, desires etc., to whom all sentient and non-sentient things are subservient and who is the support of the worlds.Further Sri Ramanuja says that the Lord is his father, mother, wealth, teacher and everything. He further asks the Lord to forgive his sins committed against the Lord and His devotees in the past, present and likely to occur in future. The true nature of the Lord is hidden by his Maya [illusion] and leads us towards objects of pleasure. [This illusion can be removed when one realises that the body is different from the soul]. Sri Ramanuja wants to serve the God through intense devotion, by acquiring knowledge, as Sri Krishna considers them as His greatest devotees. This state is acquired after countless births.

Sri Ranganatha then accepts Sri Ramanuja as His eternal servant, as he had uttered Dwaiya Mantra [worship of the Lord together with His consort] and had disassociated from attachment to the body[1], inspite of not possessing the required qualities due to innumerable sins committed against the Lord and His devotees. The Lord assures that by totally surrendering oneself to the Lord, a person experiences intense joy of serving the Lord at all times, as all his sins are destroyed and there should be no misgivings in this regard [The current prayer may be taken as the prayer uttered in the dying moment].

2. SRIRANGA GADYAM OR TEXT OF SRI RANGANATHA OF SRIRANGAM

Sri Ramanuja then addresses the Lord of Srirangam, as the one who has control over three kinds of conscious entities [those in worldly existence or bondage, those who were earlier in bondage and then got liberated and those who are eternally liberated] as well as the unconscious entity [Prakriti or matter] and who possesses innumerable auspicious qualities like strength, compassion, kindness, prowess etc., meant to protect His devotees who have sought His shelter, to accept him as eternal servant without any desires and thereby derive excessive joy of experiencing Him, inspite of his not possessing the requisite qualities [like having the knowledge of soul and supersoul], as he is bound in worldly existence.

3. SRIVAIKUNTA GADYAM OR TEXT OF SRIVAIKUNTA

Sri Ramanuja once again stresses that total surrender to the Lord will lead a devotee to Vaikunta, the land of eternal bliss. Vaikunta Loka, which is beyond the 14 known Lokas, is full of divine gardens, ponds and lakes with pure crystal water and has a divine palace studded with gem pillars. The gardens are full of fragrant fruits and flowers with birds singing melodiously, exclusively meant for the use of Lord Narayana, who is seated on Adishesha with His consort Sri [Lakshmi] and served by Garuda, Adishesha, Viswaksena[2] etc.

The Lord who illuminates the entire Universe has a radiant smile, tender cheeks and has palms adorned with conch, discus, shield, mace, sword and bow. He has eyes like the lotus flower, youthful grace and His earrings are resting on His broad shoulders. He has a mole called Srivatsa, adorned with crowns and has a chest jewel called Kausthuba. He wears yellow silk robes, and has golden waist belt and anklets and a garland known as Vyjayanthi, which never fades.

The devotee then begs the Lord, who is his father, mother, teacher, relative etc., to give him an opportunity to serve Him, without thinking of anything else, by chanting "Salutations to Lord Narayana". The Lord who is full of love and compassion, blesses the devotee by His divine glance and placing His feet on the devotee's head. The Lord then accepts the devotee as His servant, thereby removing all his miseries and giving him eternal bliss. The devotee should then bow to Him with utmost respect.

Nithyagrantham is a form of worship of the Lord, adorned with weapons, along with Nithyasooris. [Detailed method of worship is given various texts on Nithyagrantham.

END NOTES

1. Bodily association produces sorrow caused [1] due to our thinking or Adhyatma [2] by other beings or Adhibhoutika and [3] by nature or Adhidaivika.
2. Viswaksena is entrusted with the duties of creation, sustenance and destruction by the Lord.

CHAPTER - 6

SRIVACHANA BHUSHANAM
[ORNAMENT OF SAYINGS]

INTRODUCTION:

As per Pillai Lokacharya, a Bhagavatha [devotee of God] should be honoured without caste discrimination. Further the soul's objective of attaining the Lord is through the Acharya [preceptor]. The Lord Himself takes the role of Acharya, by His teachings to Arjuna [Bhagavad Gita]. Acharya is the one, who teaches the holy Astaksara Mantra "Om Namo Narayana", which relieves the soul from bondage. However, among the Alvars, only Madhurakavi had an Acharya [Nammalvar].

Pillai Lokacharya further says that the Lord is the means and the goal to be attained, while the Goddess acts as a mediator between the Lord and the soul. The Lord is concerned with souls caught in Samsara [worldly pleasures]. He thinks of rescuing the soul from bondage by every possible means. His Arcavatara [form of the Lord in images] makes the soul come closer to the Lord, while Ahankara [pride] and karma [works] makes the soul's attainment of Lord difficult. Even though the soul has qualities like knowledge and bliss, its essential nature is Sesatva [subservience] to the Lord, who is the Sesi [master]. However, karma [works] prevents the soul from reaching the Lord.

Prapatti [surrendering oneself to the Lord] is applicable to all souls irrespective of knowledge, place, time, circumstances etc. Examples: Gajendra, Jatayu, Vibhishana, Draupadi etc. The Lord is always waiting for an opportunity or excuse to rescue a soul, though the soul may turn away from Him. Even unintended visit to a temple [a person passing through a temple accidentally, while his intention was to visit some other place] wins His grace. Those who surrender should be free from pride and refrain from pleasures [like illicit sexual relations, non-violence, non-stealing, non-lying, grasping other's wives], without causing offence to Bhagavathas [devotees]. A true Bhagavatha is not determined by name, caste, family etc. but is based solely on his relationship with the Lord. Examples, of birth of low caste and non-humans graced by the Lord include Vidura, Sabari, Jatayu etc. Even Lord Krishna and Nammalvar do not belong to high caste.

As per Pillai Lokacharya, one should look at the Arca form of the Lord or the Acharya for salvation. However, the Alvars seek to protect the Lord, an inappropriate action for a Sesa. For example, Guha trying to protect Lord Rama. The Alvars also speak of divine love towards the Lord. Sri Ramanuja, who lived prior to Pillai Lokacharya, says that for a soul chosen by the Lord, to enjoy the Lord, intense devotion in the form of meditation, supported by certain works [karma] is needed. Lord chooses one who is extremely dear to Him by his devotion. However Pillai Lokacharya differs in saying that the goal of the soul is service to the Lord and surrendering to the Lord, opening the way for salvation to all persons.

CHAPTER - 7

SRIVACHANA BHUSHANAM

Ramayana focusses on Goddess Sita, while the focus of Mahabharata is Lord Krishna.

Goddess Sita, whose essential qualities are mercy, dependence on the Lord and subservience to the Lord, acts as a mediator between the soul and the Lord, when the Lord desires to punish the soul, on account of karma [evil deeds]. By not adhering to Hanuman's request to annihilate the demonesses, she exercises mercy, overlooking the defects. The Lord, in His role as the preceptor [Acharya], while preaching Arjuna, acts both as a mediator as well as the means to salvation, disregarding the soul's defects [attachment to relatives is considered as a defect], thereby enabling the Lord to accept the soul.

For Prapatti [surrender], presence of Lord in images is the only object, without condition of place, time, manner, fitness or fruit, in the manner done by the Alvars. In the Arcavatara, the Lord cares even to those who are indifferent to Him [distracted by other objects], thereby serving as a means for salvation. Three types of persons are fit to surrender in the Arca form, the ignorant persons, persons who have great knowledge [like Acharya Ramanuja] and those who are highly devoted like the Alvars. [qualities of non-sentient, sentient and related to the Lord respectively], where the Lord is both the means and the end for salvation. Sometimes the Alvars do things not conforming Prapatti, captivated by the divine attributes of the Lord [like turning away from Him when He delays in appearing due to sheer devotion]. Thus, their actions are not in contradiction to Prapatti. The only requirement for Prapatti is to serve the Lord [sesa], while the Lord is the sesi.

Sentient beings differ from non-sentient beings as they attain the Lord by constant remembrance [one of the means of attainment]. The helpless condition of a girl constantly thinking of the Lord is mentioned in PeriyaTirumoli of Tirumangai Alvar. The thought should be on the Lord, without contact with women, as well as avoiding pleasures through our five senses, as per Tiruandadi and Tiruvaimoli. By keeping the senses under control and reciting the holy Ashtakshari mantra, the Lord, as well as worldly prosperity can be attained through an Acharya [preceptor], as per Tiruvaimoli. Such persons abstain from pleasures, being caught in the beauty and grace of the Lord, which even the scriptures prescribe. The Lord effects the attainment of soul towards Him for His enjoyment. The distinguishing and natural quality of the soul from the Lord is servanthood [sesatva], though it has other qualities like knowledge and bliss, which manifests itself, when the bonds caused by pride [ahankara] is broken. Goddess Sita and Draupadi took shelter in the Lord, which is also a means of attainment, though the Goddess could have got rid of imprisonment by her own efforts. Lakshmana attained the Lord by serving Him. Some, like Jatayu, renounced their bodies in loving service of the Lord and attained the goal of salvation [Upeya].

The soul's essential nature makes it attracted towards the Lord. The Alvars speak of servitude to the Lord, even though the Lord is indifferent. The means adopted other than the Lord are mixed with pride [ahankara] and dangerous to the soul's essential nature. As everything belongs to the Lord, there is nothing which the soul can give to the Lord. Prapatti is easy to practise, since it is accompanied by renunciation alone [thinking of the Lord alone] and no other means as prescribed in the scriptures. By so doing the Lord is pleased. By offering fruits, leaf, flower or even water, with devotion, the Lord is pleased [Bhagavadgita 9.26]. However, the soul attains the Lord by the grace of the Lord. Both the soul and the Lord need a mediator. [the soul's fear of going to the Lord with all the faults and the Lord finding it difficult to accept the soul with all the faults]. Goddess [Sri] acts as a mediator for both. When there is mutual love between the soul and the Lord, the Lord takes the soul along with the body, seeing no defects in the soul [like a Jnani, a person of knowledge]. Such persons live in this world as per the Lord's wishes. The Lord loves His abode in temples, as it is through these temples that He first made contact with the soul, thereby residing in his heart. There is no goodness in the soul without the Lord. A person perishes, thinking that there is happiness in sensory objects, without the experience of the Lord.

Pride and sensuality not only destroys the essential nature of the soul, but also produces hostility to those who are devotees of the Lord [Bhagavathas]. Fake Bhagavathas, calling themselves Bhagavathas, who create trouble for true Bhagavathas, get destroyed. The incarnations of the Lord show that the Lord does not tolerate offence to Bhagavathas. Sri

Krishna advises Yudhisthira to treat the Bhagavathas with the same affection, as shown towards Him.

Questioning a Bhagavatha's birth as well as offending the Bhagavathas will lead to destruction. However offences to Bhagavathas are condoned by repentance.

A high-born person must cultivate humility. A low-born devoted person is higher than a high-born person of learning, without devotion.

By associating with a Bhagavatha, a person develops Bhakti. Thus, a Bhagavatha, though of low birth is equal to an Acharya. Eg: Sri Rama performing funeral rites, as applicable to Brahmins, for Jatayu. Sri Krishna and Sri Rama taking food in Vidura's and Sabari's abode respectively.

A devotee, free from pride and sensuous pleasures, attains the lotus feet of the Lord.

Mangalasasana or prayer is appropriate for the inferior Sesha towards the superior Sesin [Lord], as it is an expression of love. Eg: Perialvar, who always thought of holy places without food or sleep, invoking protection to the Lord, who had no one to sympathise.

A person's mere association with true and knowledgeable devotees, who have renounced everything, is enough for him to acquire those virtues.

Those who are addicted to worldly enjoyments and worship other Gods cannot attain the Lord. The Lord must be experienced by the grace of the Acharya [or mediator] rather than by one's own experience. The devotees should make offerings to the Lord for His acceptance, just as Vidura offering food, flower- maker [malakara] offering flowers and hunch back offering sandal paste. [the only means of the ignorant and imperfect soul being freed from samsara is the attainment of the Lord].

Affront is [1] doing forbidden acts like illegal sex, taking prohibited food, violence and speaking untruth [2] not believing in God [3] criticizing devotees due to pride and worldliness.

Attainment of the Lord should be the aim of all mantras [sacred utterances]. If it is used otherwise, it will result in bondage.

The disciple is indebted to his preceptor to such an extent, that he cannot repay the debt. The preceptor gets pleased when a disciple enjoys the Lord by reciting the mantra and finally showing gratitude to the preceptor and the Lord. The preceptor should not instruct those who are not qualified [not believing in God]. He should also not give wrong meanings of the mantra.

The mind of the soul that considers defect in the Lord and the Bhagavathas is considered to be evil. A person should not speak ill of even those who are sinful, like Goddess Sita pardoning the demonesses.

Thinking of one's fault, there is fear and thinking of the virtues of the Lord there is fearlessness. An ignorant person sees virtue in his self and defects in the Lord.

The cause of salvation is Lord's grace, bondage is due to soul's fault. [the soul should not accuse the Lord of causing bondage]. However there is escape for the soul's fault by surrendering at the Lord's feet. Eg: Lord Rama pardoning the crow, which deserved to be killed.

The Lord is constantly thinking of those who are in bondage and tries to rescue them from bondage by every possible means. Even unintentional good deeds form the basis of Lord's grace. The Alvars express gratitude to the Lord, for having graced them [by their constantly thinking and serving Him], without any expectation. The soul's very sight of the Lord makes way for salvation. [merits and demerits of the soul being extinguished]. As per the Alvars , the Lord's incarnations in different periods is to sing the hymns, praising His qualities. The Lord's abundant grace, which none can stop is the cause of fearlessness, while Karma is the cause of fear. Fear and fearlessness will persist till the attainment of the Lord.

The Acharya serves both the soul and the Lord. The Alvars speak of the Lord being merciful as well as non-merciful. The Lord being without mercy is due to the fault of the soul alone. The soul accepts the Lord appearing with defects or without defects, as the relationship is a natural one. The Lord himself takes the role of Acharya by teaching the Gita. Since the attainment of the Lord is through an Acharya, it is impossible to repay the Acharya. The soul's essential nature blossoms when it is in relationship with the Acharya. Associating with devotees [Bhagavathas] helps one attain Acharya. Those who do not depend on the Acharya and worship other Gods go against the soul. By faulting theAcharya, the Lord and the Bhagavathas, a soul gets destroyed.

Unlawful sexual enjoyment is condemned by the world and is the cause of hell. However, even lawful sexual enjoyment is to be renounced as it is opposed to the essential nature of the vedanta and is an hindrance to attainment.

The four means of salvation are Bhakti, Prapatti, obtaining grace of the Lord with efforts and without efforts [purely by the grace of the Lord]. Humility destroys the sins and is the gateway to salvation. Humans, animals or birds, by associating with true devotees, will enjoy Vaikunta.

Praising the Bhagavathas has greater merit than praising the Lord without an Acharya.

CHAPTER - 8

POWER OF SAGES

Wealth of Powers of our Ancient Sages

1. Sage Ayoda Dhaumya blessed his disciple Aruni [Uddalaka] with good fortune as well as having the knowledge of vedas for having stopped a breach in the watercourse by lying himself there. [Mahabharata Adi Parva Paushya Parva Sec III].

Another disciple Upamanyu, who lost his eyesight, while obeying his preceptor's command regained his sight by propitiating the Aswins [physicians of Gods], as per his preceptor's instructions. [Mahabharata Adi Parva Paushya Parva Sec III].

Sage Ayoda Dhaumya's disciple Veda had a disciple by name Utanka, and he gave a pair of earrings, obtained from King Paushya's queen, to his preceptor's wife, as honorarium for his preceptor, even though it was seized by the Naga Takshaka and hid in the nether regions, by his preceptor's grace. [Mahabharata Adi Parva Paushya Parva Sec III].

2. Even as a child Sage Chyavana [son of Sage Bhrigu] rescued his mother from a Rakshasa, by burning him to ashes. Pauloma, who was carrying the baby [Sage Chyavana] and abducted by the Rakshasa [demon], with whom she was originally engaged, was identified by Agni, God of fire. Agni, for this act was cursed by Sage Bhrigu to eat [consume] all things [pure and impure].[Mahabharata Adi Parva Pauloma Parva Sec Vand VI].

3. The royal sage Ruru was able to revive his wife, bitten by a snake, by giving half his life. [Mahabharata Adi Parva Pauloma Parva Sec IX].

The very sight of royal sage Ruru caused Dundubha attain his original form, from the serpentine form, which he had obtained due to a curse. [Mahabharata Adi Parva Pauloma Parva Sec XI].

4. When King Parikshit threw a dead snake at the shoulder of Sage Sameeka, his son Sringin cursed Parikshit to be bitten by the Naga Takshaka, within seven days. [Mahabharata AdiParva Astika Parva Sec XLI]. [the sage who was in meditation did not provide water to the thirsty Parikshit].

5. Sage Sukra used to revive the dead with the knowledge of science called Sanjivini. [Mahabharata AdiParva Sambhava Parva Sec LXXVI]

When King Yayati married a second time [Devayani, daughter of Sage Sukra was his first wife], Sage Sukra cursed Yayati with old age. [Mahabharata AdiParva Sambhava Parva Sec LXXXIII].

6. Sathyavati, wife of King Santanu begot Vichitravirya, who died young. So in order to continue the lineage, she requested her other son sage Vyasa to beget progeny through Ambika and Ambalika, wives of King Vichitravirya. By the mere sight of sage Vyasa, Ambika begot Dritarashtra and Ambalika, king Pandu. [Mahabharata AdiParva Sambhava Parva Sec CVI].

7. When Sage Mandavya was severely punished by a king for a minor offence, he asked Yama, the reason for the same. Yama replied that he had suffered due to the sin of killing an insect in his twelfth year, earlier. The sage cursed Yama to be born on earth in a lower order, as a wrong committed by a person upto the twelfth year can be condoned.[Mahabharata AdiParva Sambhava Parva Sec CVIII]].

8. Sage Durvasa, pleased with the service rendered by Kunti, when he visited her father's house, gave her a boon of begetting children through celestials, by reciting certain mantras. [Mahabharata AdiParva Sambhava Parva Sec CXI]

9. Sage Vyasa, pleased with Gandhari's hospitality, blessed that she would have a century of sons. [Mahabharata AdiParva Sambhava Parva Sec CXV].

10. King Pandu, who accidentally killed a sage's son of great ascetic merit while he was mating in the form of a deer, was cursed that he [King Pandu] would meet with his end, if he mates with his wife lustfully. [Mahabharata AdiParva Sambhava Parva Sec CXVIII].

11. Sage Sakthi, son of sage Vasistha, who was whipped by King Kalmashapada, for blocking his way, cursed the king to be a rakshasa. [Mahabharata AdiParva Chaitraratha Parva Sec CLXXVIII].

12. When Indra did not pour rain during sage Agastya's sacrifice, the sage by virtue of his penances made Indra pour rain. [Mahabharata Aswamedha Parva Anugita Parva Sec XCII].

13. King Dhritarashtra and the Pandavas could see their kinsmen killed in battle for one night, by the grace of Sage Vyasa. They then proceeded to their respective abodes in heaven. Dritarashtra also got his eyesight to behold his sons etc for one night by the grace of sage Vyasa. [Mahabharata Asramavasika Parva Putradarsana Parva Sec XXXII].

Similarly, Janamejaya could behold his father Parikshit in the same form, as he was prior to his departure to the other world by the grace of Sage Vyasa. [Mahabharata Asramavasika Parva Putradarsana Parva Sec XXXV].

14. The haughty Vrishnis [tribe of Sri Krishna], dressing Samba, son of Sri Krishna, like a woman, asked the sages whether he would deliver a boy or a girl, to which the sages replied that he would bring forth an iron rod, which would be the cause of destruction of Vrishni clan and thus the Vrishni's were destroyed. [Mahabharata Mausala Parva Sec 1]

15. By marrying Sage Galava's son Sringavat, an old and infirm lady [she married on the advice of Sage Narada], became young. By virtue of her ascetic penances and this marriage, she attained heaven. [Mahabharata Shalya Parva Sec 52].

16. When the lustful Nahusha kicked Agastya, who was carrying the palanquin along with the other sages, the sage cursed him to be a snake. [Mahabharata Udyoga Parva Sec XVII]

17. Sage Maitreya cursed Duryodhana that Bhima would smash his thighs in the great war, for being slighted by Duryodhana. [Mahabharata Vana Parva Aranyaka Parva Sec X].

18. Ilwala, the Asura, killed many holy sages, by making a meat of his brother Vatapi and asking him to come out of their stomachs. However, Sage Agastya digested the AsuraVatapi, when Ilwala tried to play the trick on him. [Mahabharata Vana Parva Tirtha Yatra Parva Sec XCIX].

19. Indra, the king of Gods was able to slay Vrita, the great Asura [demon], with the thunderbolt made from the bones of sage Dadichi. [Mahabharata Vana Parva Tirtha Yatra Parva Sec C].

20. Once Vindhya mountains began to grow tall in order to compete with Mt. Meru. However, it shrunk in size to give way to sage Agastya, who stood in front of him. The sage asked the mountain Vindhya to remain in that position till he returned from south, which he never did. [Canopus, a southern constellation star is identified with sage Agastya].[Vana Parva Sec CIV]

Sage Agastya drunk the sea water, as per the wishes of Gods, as a large number of demons called Kalakeyas were hiding in it. However, it was replenished later by king Bhagirath's penance. [Mahabharata Vana Parva Tirtha Yatra Parva Sec CV]

21. During the penance of sage Vibhandaka, he beheld celestial nymph Urvashi, whereupon came his seminal fluid. A hind [daughter of Gods], which drank the fluid along with water, conceived sage Rishyasringa. As foretold by Brahma, the hind proceeded to the world of gods after the birth of sage Rishyasringa. [Mahabharata Vana Parva Tirtha Yatra Parva Sec X].

By the mere presence of sage Rishyasringa, there occurred heavy rainfall in the land of Lomapada, which was hitherto devoid of rains. [Mahabharata Vana Parva Tirtha Yatra Parva CX to CXIII].

22. When sage Richika wanted to marry the daughter of Gadhi of lunar dynasty [Satyavati], Gadhi demanded 1000 white horses with one blue ear, as dowry for his daughter. Sage Richika obtained the horses as described from Varuna and thus married Satyavati. [Srimad Bhagavatam canto 9 chapter 15].

23. When sage Chyavana wanted to make an offering of Soma juice to the Aswins [physician of the celestials] in a sacrifice, Indra, the king of gods, objected saying that the Aswins were not entitled to Soma juice. He tried to hurl his thunderbolt at sage Chyavana, who then paralysed his arm. Indra, then permitted sage Chyavana to offer soma juice to the Aswins. [Mahabharata Vana Parva Tirtha Yatra Parva Sec CXXIV and V]

24. Ashtavakra [born with eight crooked limbs as per his father Kahoda's curse, as Kahoda's mistakes, while reciting shastras, were pointed by Ashtavakra, even while Ashtavakra was in his mother's womb] defeated Vandin [Vandin caused Kahoda to drown in a river, after Kahoda was defeated in debate]. Vandin entered the sea but Kahoda sprang to life owing to Ashtavakra's spiritual knowledge. Ashtavakra's crooked limbs got straightened after his father blessed him and asked him to bathe in river Samanga. [Mahabharata Vana Parva Tirtha Yatra Parva Sec CXXXII to IV].

25. When sage Yavakri, son of sage Bharadwaja cast lustful eyes on the daughter-in-law of sage Raivya, sage Raivya cursed him to die. Sage Bharadwaja then cursed Raiva, that the cause of his death would be one of his sons [Paravasu] and died entering the fire. But Paravasu put the blame on his brother Aravasu. However, Aravasu, by virtue of his penances and good conduct restored to life the slain Bharadwaja, his son Yavakri and his own father Raivya, absolving his brother of the sin of killing his father. Further Raivya did not have the memory of his being slain by virtue of Aravasu's penance. [Mahabharata Vana Parva Tirtha Yatra Parva Sec CXXXVII and CXXXVIII].

26. Sage Valadhi had obtained a boon from the Gods that his son, Medhavin was to die only after the destruction of the mountains. [as mountains could not be destroyed, the sage thought that his son would be immortal]. Medhavin, learning of the incident grew haughty and troubled the sages. However, one sage, Dhannushaksha, caused the mountain to be shattered by buffaloes and thus Medhavin was slain. [Mahabharata Vana Parva Tirtha Yatra Parva Sec CXXXV].

27. When the lustful Indra, the king of Gods made advances towards sage Devasarman's wife [in the absence of the sage], she was protected by the disciple of Devasarman [Vipula], who entered her body and made Indra flee from the spot. [Mahabharata Anusasana Parva Sec XLI].

28. When sage Chyavana was caught by fishermen along with other fishes and the price of Chyavana was paid to fishermen [value of cow] by the king, the sage blessed the fishermen and fishes to ascend heaven. [Mahabharata Anusasana Parva Sec L].

29. When Goddess Earth went to the region of Brahman, displeased with king Anga presenting her to holy men [Brahmanas], sage Kashyapa entered her body and discharged her functions till she returned from the region of Brahman. [Mahabharata Anusasana Parva Sec CLIV].

30. When Bhadra, daughter of moon-deity and wife of sage Utathya of Angiras lineage was abducted by Varuna [God of water], sage Utathya drank the water and made river Saraswathi invisible. Finally Varuna returned Bhadra to sage Utathya.[Mahabharata Anusasana Parva Sec CLIV].

31. Once when the Gods were defeated by Asuras, sage Agastya burnt the Asuras by the wealth of his penances. [MahabharataAnusasanaParva Sec CLV].

Similarly sageVasistha rescued the Gods from the Danavas, who had taken refuge in a lake, by destroying them.[Mahabharata Anusasana Parva Sec CLV].

32. Once sage Atri, assuming the form of Soma [moon-deity] and Surya [sun-deity] destroyed the Danavas. Further when Soma and Surya lost their lustre, sage Atri made the Universe shine.[Mahabharata Anusasana Parva Sec CLVI].

33. Talajangala, a Kshatriya was destroyed by sage Aurva.[Mahabharata Anusasana Parva Sec CLIII].

34. When a class of beings called kapas usurped heaven after defeating the Gods, they were burnt by the fires created by the Brahmanas [holy men]..[Mahabharata Anusasana Parva Sec CLVII].

35. Once sage Durvasa stayed in Sri Krishna's palace and did horrible things like burning all beds, beating Goddess Rukmani, while yoking her to a car etc. However, the Goddess felt no pain afterwards and the burnt things were restored. Sage Durvasa then blessed Lord Krishna and His principal consort, Goddess Rukmani. [Mahabharata Anusasana Parva Sec CLIX].

Sage Chyavana, while staying in the kingdom of Kusika, made the king and queen press his feet while he was awake, rub his body with oil, carry him on a palanquin while beating them with goad, gave away precious jewels etc while going on palanquin etc. Sage Chyavana blessed the king saying that a person [Viswamitra], who though born in the lineage of Kusika, would attain Brahmanhood, being the equal of Brihaspati, the preceptor of celestials..[Mahabharata Anusasana Parva Sec LII to LVI].

36. When Likhita stole fruits in his brother Sankha's garden, Sankha asked his brother to apprise the king of the theft. Accordingly Likhita went to the king, who on hearing of the incident ordered Likhita's hands to be cut off. Sankha then asked Likhita to bathe in a sacred river with oblations to Gods, sages and Pitrus [ancestors], when the two hands of Likhita reemerged. Such was Sankha's power of penance. [Mahabharata Santi Parva Raja Dharmanusana Parva Sec XXIII].

37. Once sages Narada and Parvata [Narada,s sister's son] came to earth and resided in King Srinjaya's palace, with an understanding that no secret should be kept within themselves. However, sage Narada failed to inform Parvata about his love affair with the king's daughter, to which Parvata cursed Narada to have an ape's face. Narada in turn cursed Parvata, that he would not be able to ascend heaven. However, when Parvata wanted Narada to withdraw the curse, Narada also asked Parvata to do the same. Thus, both Narada and Parvata were freed from the curses. [Mahabharata Santi Parva Rajadharmanusana Parva Sec XXX].

When sage Parvata blessed King Srinjaya that a child who would outwit Indra would be born to him, Indra grew anxious and therefore slew the child with his thunderbolt, which took the form of a tiger. The grieving king thought of sage Narada, who revived the child. [Mahabharata Santi Parva Rajadharmanusana Parva Sec XXXI].

38. Lord Narayana blessed sage Vyasa with the knowledge of the past, present and future.[Mahabharata Santi Parva Sec CCCL]

39. By the mere grace of sage Viswamitra, drought which prevailed in Ayodhya for 12 years was removed. [Mahabharata Santi Parva Apadharmanusasana Parva Sec CXLI].

40. Sage Garga performed austerities for 12 years consuming only iron powder. [Harivamsapurana Vishnuparva Chapter 52].

41. Sri Rama and Lakshmana were instructed with mantras known as Bala and Atibala by sage Vishwamitra, which frees a person from fatigue, fever etc. [Valmiki Ramayana, Bala Kanda, Canto 22].

42. Kusanabha's [in whose lineage was born Viswamitra], daughter's who were deformed by wind-god [who got angry for not marrying him] were cured of the deformity by sage Brahmadatta, who married them. [Valmiki Ramayana Bala Kanda Canto 33].

43. When Indra, the king of Gods had illegal sex with the wife of the sage Gautama [Ahalya], the sage cursed Indra to be deprived of his testicles. Further the sage cursed Ahalya to live on air alone, till she received Sri Rama's blessings, when he sets his foot in the hermitage. [Valmiki Ramayana Bala Kanda Canto 48].

44. When Viswamitra tried to forcefully snatch the wish-yielding cow of Vasistha, by discharging celestial missiles on Vasistha, Vasistha by means of his brahmanical staff alone withstood all those missiles. [Valmiki Ramayana Bala Kanda Chapter 56]

45. Sage Viswamitra, by the power of his austerities made King Trisanku bodily ascend heaven and on the Gods refusal to accept him, created constellations in the Southern quarter, where Trisanku exists even today. [Valmiki Ramayana Bala Kanda Canto 60].

46. Sage Vasistha's sons, who refused to attend the sacrifice of sage Vishwamitra, were reduced to ashes by Vishwamitra's power of austerities. [Valmiki Ramayana Bala Kanda Chapter 59]

47. When Sunahsepa was offered as a sacrificial beast by King Ambarisha [Harishchandra], the dieties pleased with the mantras recited by Sunahsepa, taught by sage Vishwamitra, granted him long life.[Srimad Bhagavatam Canto 9 Chapter 16]

48. The Gods with Indra came to the hermitage of sage Sarabhanga to take him to Brahmaloka, abode of Brahma, the creator.[Valmiki Ramayana Aranyakanda canto 5].

49. While Sri Rama was in the forest, sage Agastya gave Him a bow of Visshnu, along with divine missiles. [Valmiki Ramayana Aranyakanda canto 12].

50. When Vali, the king of monkeys killed the demon Dhundubhi, blood drops fell on the hermitage of sage Matanga, who cursed Vali to die instantaneously, if he entered the vicinity of his hermitage. [Valmiki Ramayana Kishkindakanda canto 11].

51. By virtue of their austerities, the seven sages called as Saptajanas bodily ascended heaven. [Valmiki Ramayana Kishkindakanda canto XIII].

52. Sage Kandu, who lost his 10 year old son cursed the area to be devoid of animals and plants. [Valmiki Ramayana Kishkindakanda Chapter 48].

53. The monkeys led by Hanuman, who had gone in search of Sita, entered a cave consisting of delicious fruits. They were able to come out of the cave only by the power of austerities of Swayamprabha, the ascetic woman.[Valmiki Ramayana Kishkindakanda canto 52].

54. Sage Agastya advises Sri Rama to recite a hymn in praise of the Sun God, by which he would be able to conquer his enemies. [Valmiki Ramayana Yuddha Kanda chapter 105].

55. When sage Parasara's father was killed by a demon [rakshasa], the sage performed a rite, in which hundreds of rakshasas were killed. However, the sage's grandfather Vasistha advised the sage to desist from killing the rakshasas further.[Mahabharata AdiParva Chaitraratha Parva Sec CLXXXIII].

56. Sage Saubhari, though old in age, transformed himself into a youth and desiring family life, married 50 daughters of King Mandhata and lead a happy life with them simultaneously. However, he then started living a life of detachment, meditating on Lord Vishnu, seeking salvation. [Srimad Bhagavatam canto 9 chapter 6].

57. When King Nimi, son of Ikshvaku, engaged the services of sage Gautama in a sacrifice [the family priest sage Vasistha could not immediately participate in the sacrifice due to pre-occupation], sage Vasistha cursed Nimi, to lose his bodily form. Nimi in turn cursed sage Vasistha. The Gods blessed Nimi that he would be present in the eyelids of all living beings [when the eyelids open and close], as Nimi did not want to live with a body.[Srimad Bhagavatam canto 9 chapter 13].

58. Sage Narada could remember his past birth of being the son of a maid-servant [Srimad Bhagavatam canto 1 chapter 5].

59. When Diti, wife of sage Kashyapa wanted to have sex with her husband during evening time [forbidden time], the sage cursed that she would give birth to two sons, who would be the terror of the worlds. Further they would be killed by Mahavishnu, in order to protect the Universe. [Srimad Bhagavatam canto 3 chapter 14].

When the Sanaka sages were prevented from having a Darshan [vision] of the Lord, by his two attendants, Jaya and Vijaya, the sages cursed them to be born on earth. [Srimad Bhagavatam canto 3 chapter 15].

60. King Vena was killed by the sages by invoking a hymn, for his misrule and also for insulting Mahavishnu. When the sages churned the arms of Vena, King Prithu and queen Archis, parts of Mahavishnu and Mahalakshmi respectively, emerged. [Srimad Bhagavatam canto 4 chapters 14, 15].

61. By the grace of Sage Angiras, King Chitrakethu bore a son through his senior queen. [the sage performed a sacrifice and the remnant was given to the queen]. However, the child was poisoned to death by his other wives. When sage Narada spoke to the soul of the dead child, in the presence of sorrowing relatives, the soul replied that it was not interested in entering the body of the child and departed. [Srimad Bhagavatam can to 6, chapters 14,15,16].

62. When Indra treated sage Durvasa disrespectfully, the sage cursed Indra to lose the sovereignty of the three worlds. [Srimad Bhagavatam canto 8 chapter 5]

Mahabali, with the blessings of sage Sukra, was able to conquer Indra and the Gods. [Srimad Bhagavatam canto 8 chapter 15]

63. King Yuvanasva, who was childless, requested the sages for progeny. The sages performed a sacrificial rite and placing the consecrated water upon the altar, retired. When King Yuvanasva accidentally cosumed the holy water, after feeling thirsty, a child sprang forth bursting the king's abdomen. The child was then fed by Indra and given the name Mandhata. [Srimad Bhagavatam canto 9 chapter 6].

64. Sage Richika, who married the daughter of Gadhi by name Sathyavathi, prepared two separate dishes, one for Sathyavathi and the other for her mother, for begetting children. However, without the sage's knowledge, Sathyavathi consumed the dish meant for her mother, while her mother consumed the dish meant for Sathyavathi. When sage Richika came to know of it, he said that the son, who would be born to Sathyavathi ,would be the terror of the worlds. When the sage was requested by Sathyavathi that it should not happen, the sage said that the grandson of Sathyavathi [Parasurama] would be the terror of the worlds. Thus, the sage could modify an event bound to happen as per sacrificial rites. [Srimad Bhagavatam canto 9 chapter 15].

65. During the naming ceremony of Balarama and Sri Krishna in secrecy, sage Garga revealed the divinity of Balarama and Sri Krishna. [Srimad Bhagavatam canto 10 chapter 8].

66. King Nriga gave a cow he had gifted to a holy man [brahmana] originally to another holy man, as the cow had accidentally strayed back into the herd. Both the holy men contended that the cow was given to them by the king and the king was punished by Yama, converting him into a lizard. [Srimad Bhagavatam canto 10 chapter 64].

67. Sage Markandeya experienced the events happening during deluge, when Lord Mahavishnu was requested by the sage to shown his mystic power. [only the sage's personal experience and hence not universal]. [Srimad Bhagavatam canto 12 chapter 9].

68. Sage Jaratkaru married the sister of Naga Vasuki, who had the same name Jaratkaru and begot in her sage Astika, who saved the snakes from falling in the fire. [the snake sacrifice was performed by King Janamejaya to avenge the death of his father Parikshit at the hands of the Naga, Takshaka]. [Mahabharata Adi Parva Astika Parva Sec XLVII and XLVIII].

CHAPTER - 9

108 DIVYA DESHAM

Significance of 108:

The no. is roughly the distance of the sun from earth in terms of sun's diameter.

Sun's diameter is 864948.7 miles. Distance from sun to earth is 92.96 million miles. 864948.7 * 107.6 = 93.06 million miles. [roughly 92.96 million miles] –A

It is also roughly the average distance from moon to earth in terms of moon's diameter.

Moon's diameter is 2159 miles.

2159 * 110.6 = 238785 miles. Distance from moon to earth is 238900 miles-B

It is also roughly the diameter of sun in terms of diameter of earth.

Diameter of sun= 864948.7 miles. Diameter of earth= 7917.5 miles.

7917.5 * 109.2 = 864591 miles [roughly 864948.7 miles].

Alvars or great devotees of the lord:

There are 12 Alvars as per tradition. They are:

1. Poigai Alvar
2. Boothath Alvar
3. Pei Alvar
4. Thirumalishai Alvar
5. Kulashekar Alvar
6. Peri Alvar
7. Andal
8. Thondaripudi Alvar
9. Thirupann Alvar
10. Thirumangai Alvar
11. Namm Alvar
12. Madhurakavi Alvar.

The 108 Divya Deshams [sacred places] as per Vaishnava tradition, have become sacred due to hymns sung by the 12 Alvars mentioned above.

The 108 Divya Deshams and the hymns sung by the Alvar/Alwars corresponding to the Divya Desham, is given below:

S.N.	Name of Divya Desham	Located in	Hymns sung by
1	Tanjai Mamani koil	Tamilnadu [Tanjore-Kumbakonam belt]	Thirumangai Alvar, Boothath Alvar
2	Thirukandiyur	Tamilnadu	Thirumangai Alvar
3	Thirukudalur	Tamilnadu [Tanjore-Kumbakonam belt]	Thirumangai Alvar
4	Thirukkavittalam [Kapisthalam]	Tamilnadu [Tanjore-Kumbakonam belt]	Thirumangai Alvar, Thirumalishai Alvar
5	Thirupullam Buthangudi	Tamilnadu [Tanjore-Kumbakonam belt]	Thirumangai Alvar
6	Thiruadanur	Tamilnadu [Tanjore-Kumbakonam belt]	Thirumangai Alvar
7	Thirukudandai	Tamilnadu [Tanjore-Kumbakonam belt]	Peri Alvar, Andal, Thirumalishai Alvar, Thirumangai Alvar, Namm Alvar, Boothath Alvar, Pei Alvar
8	Thiruvinnagar	Tamilnadu [Tanjore-Kumbakonam belt]	Thirumangai Alvar, Namm Alvar, Pei Alvar
9	Thirunaraiyur	Tamilnadu [Tanjore-Kumbakonam belt]	Thirumangai Alvar
10	Thiruchherai	Tamilnadu [Tanjore-Kumbakonam belt]	Thirumangai Alvar
11	Thirukkanamangai	Tamilnadu [Tanjore-Kumbakonam belt]	Thirumangai Alvar
12	Thirunandipura Vinnagaram	Tamilnadu [Tanjore-Kumbakonam belt]	Thirumangai Alvar
13	Thiruvelliyamkudi	Tamilnadu [Tanjore-Kumbakonam belt]	Thirumangai Alvar
14	ThiruIndalur	Tamilnadu [Mayiladuturai belt]	Thirumangai Alvar
15	Terazhundur	Tamilnadu [Mayiladuturai belt]	Thirumangai Alvar
16	Thirusirupuliyur	Tamilnadu [Mayiladuturai belt]	Thirumangai Alvar

17	Thirukannapuram	Tamilnadu [Mayiladuturai belt]	Peri Alvar, Andal, Kulashekar Alvar, Thirumangai Alvar, Namm Alvar
18	Thirunagai	Tamilnadu [Mayiladuturai belt]	Thirumangai Alvar
19	Thirukannangudi	Tamilnadu [Mayiladuturai belt]	Thirumangai Alvar
20	Thirutalaichangaranmathe yam	Tamilnadu [Mayiladuturai belt]	Thirumangai Alvar
21	Thirukalicheerama Vinnagaram	Tamilnadu [Sirkhazhi belt]	Thirumangai Alvar
22	Thiruvellakulam [Annan koil]	Tamilnadu [Sirkhazhi belt]	Thirumangai Alvar
23	Thirudevanar Togai	Tamilnadu [Sirkhazhi belt]	Thirumangai Alvar
24	ThiruvaliTirunagari	Tamilnadu [Sirkhazhi belt]	Thirumangai Alvar
25	Thirukavalampadi	Tamilnadu [Sirkhazhi belt]	Thirumangai Alvar
26	Thirumanikudam	Tamilnadu [Sirkhazhi belt]	Thirumangai Alvar
27	Thiruparthanpalli	Tamilnadu [Sirkhazhi belt]	Thirumangai Alvar
28	Thirumanimada kovil	Tamilnadu [Sirkhazhi belt]	Thirumangai Alvar
29	Thiruarameya Vinnagaram	Tamilnadu [Sirkhazhi belt]	Thirumangai Alvar
30	Thirutetri Ambalam	Tamilnadu [Sirkhazhi belt]	Thirumangai Alvar
31	Thirusomponsai Kovil	Tamilnadu [Sirkhazhi belt]	Thirumangai Alvar
32	Thiruvan Purushotham	Tamilnadu [Sirkhazhi belt]	Thirumangai Alvar
33	Thiruvaikunda Vinnagaram	Tamilnadu [Sirkhazhi belt]	Thirumangai Alvar
35	Thirukkoli [Uraiyur]	Tamilnadu [Tiruchirapalli belt]	Thirumangai Alvar
36	Thirukarambanur	Tamilnadu [Tiruchirapalli belt]	Thirumangai Alvar
37	Thiruvellarai	Tamilnadu [Tiruchirapalli belt]	Peri Alvar, Thirumangai Alvar
38	Thiruambil	Tamilnadu [Tiruchirapalli belt]	Thirumalishai Alvar
39	Thirupper Nagar	Tamilnadu [Tiruchirapalli belt]	Peri Alvar, Thirumangai Alvar, Namm Alvar

40	Tirupati [Venkatam/Tirumala]	Andhra Pradesh	Peri Alvar, Andal, Kulashekar Alvar, Thirumalishai Alvar, Thirupann Alvar, Thirumangai Alvar, Namm Alvar, Poigai Alvar, Boothath Alvar, Pei Alvar
41	Thirusingavel Kundram [Ahobilam]	Andhra Pradesh	Thirumangai Alvar
42	Thiruchitrakutam [Chidambaram]	Tamilnadu [Cuddalore belt]	Kulashekar Alvar, Thirumangai Alvar
43	Thiruvaheendrapuram	Tamilnadu [Cuddalore belt]	Thirumangai Alvar
44	Thirukkovillur	Tamilnadu [Cuddalore belt]	Thirumangai Alvar, Pei Alvar
45	Athiyur [Thirukkachi]	Tamilnadu [Kanchipuram belt]	Boothath Alvar
46	Thiruashtabuyakaram	Tamilnadu [Kanchipuram belt]	Thirumangai Alvar
47	Thiruvehka	Tamilnadu [Kanchipuram belt]	Thirumalishai Alvar, Thirumangai Alvar, Pei Alvar, Namm Alvar
48	Thiruvelukkai	Tamilnadu [Kanchipuram belt]	Pei Alvar, Thirumangai Alvar
49	Thiruthanka	Tamilnadu [Kanchipuram belt]	Thirumangai Alvar
50	Thirukalvanur	Tamilnadu [Kanchipuram belt]	Thirumangai Alvar
51	Thiruooragam	Tamilnadu [Kanchipuram belt]	Thirumalishai Alvar, Thirumangai Alvar
52	ThiruNiragam	Tamilnadu [Kanchipuram belt]	Thirumangai Alvar
53	ThiruKaragam	Tamilnadu [Kanchipuram belt]	Thirumangai Alvar
54	Thirukarvanam	Tamilnadu [Kanchipuram belt]	Thirumangai Alvar
55	Thiruparameshwara Vinnagaram	Tamilnadu [Kanchipuram belt]	Thirumangai Alvar
56	Thiru Pavalavannan	Tamilnadu [Kanchipuram belt]	Thirumangai Alvar
57	Thiru Nilathingal Thundam	Tamilnadu [Kanchipuram belt]	Thirumangai Alvar
58	Thiru Padagam	Tamilnadu [Kanchipuram belt]	Thirumalishai Alvar, Boothath Alvar
59	Thiruputkuli	Tamilnadu [Kanchipuram belt]	Thirumangai Alvar

60	Thiruvalikkeni	Tamilnadu [Chennai belt]	Thirumangai Alvar
61	Thiruneermalai	Tamilnadu [Chennai belt]	Thirumangai Alvar
62	Thiruvedanthai	Tamilnadu [Chennai belt]	Thirumangai Alvar
63	Thirukadalmallai [Mahabalipuram]	Tamilnadu [Chennai belt]	Thirumangai Alvar, Boothath Alvar
64	Thirunindravur	Tamilnadu [Chennai belt]	Thirumangai Alvar,
65	Thiruevallur [Tiruvellore]	Tamilnadu [Chennai belt]	Thirumangai Alvar, Thirumalishai Alvar
66	Thirukkadigai [Sholinghur]	Tamilnadu [Chennai belt]	Thirumangai Alvar
67	Thirukoodal	Tamilnadu [Madurai belt]	Thirumalishai Alvar Thirumangai Alvar
68	Thirumogur	Tamilnadu [Madurai belt]	Namm Alvar, Thirumangai Alvar
69	Thirumalilansholai	Tamilnadu [Madurai belt]	Peri Alvar, Andal, Thirumangai Alvar, Namm Alvar
70	Thirukkotiyur	Tamilnadu [Madurai belt]	Peri Alvar, Thirumangai Alvar, Boothath Alvar, Pei Alvar, Thirumalishai Alvar
71	Thirumaiyam	Tamilnadu [Madurai belt]	Thirumangai Alvar
72	Thirupullani	Tamilnadu [Madurai belt]	Thirumangai Alvar
73	Thirutankal [Shivakashi]	Tamilnadu [Madurai belt]	Boothath Alvar, Thirumangai Alvar
74	Srivilliputtur	Tamilnadu [Madurai belt]	Peri Alvar, Andal
75	Thiruvaikuntam	Tamilnadu [Thirunelveli belt]	Namm Alvar
76	Thiruvaragunamangai	Tamilnadu [Thirunelveli belt]	Namm Alvar
77	Thirupullingudu	Tamilnadu [Thirunelveli belt]	Namm Alvar
78	Thirukkullanthai	Tamilnadu [Thirunelveli belt]	Namm Alvar
79	Thiruthollaivillimangalam	Tamilnadu [Thirunelveli belt]	Namm Alvar
80	Thirupperai	Tamilnadu [Thirunelveli belt]	Namm Alvar
81	Thirukkollur	Tamilnadu [Thirunelveli belt]	Namm Alvar

82	Thirukurugur [Alvar Thirunagari]	Tamilnadu [Thirunelveli belt]	Namm Alvar
83	Thiruvaramangai [Vanamamalai]	Tamilnadu [Thirunelveli belt]	Namm Alvar
84	Thirukkurungudi	Tamilnadu [Thirunelveli belt]	Peri Alvar, Thirumalishai Alvar, Thirumangai Alvar, Namm Alvar
85	Thiruvanparisaram	Tamilnadu [Thirunelveli belt]	Namm Alvar
86	Thiruvattaru	Tamilnadu [Thirunelveli belt]	Namm Alvar
87	Thiruvananthapuram	Kerala	Namm Alvar
88	Thirupuliyur [Chengannur]	Kerala	Namm Alvar
89	Thiruchenkundrur [Chengannur]	Kerala	Namm Alvar
90	Thiruvaranvillai [Arunmulla temple]	Kerala	Namm Alvar
91	Thiruvanvandur [Chengannur]	Kerala	Namm Alvar
92	Thiruvallavazh [Tiruvalla]	Kerala	Namm Alvar, Thirumangai Alvar
93	Thirukkaditanam [Changanasheri]	Kerala	Namm Alvar
94	Thirukkatarai [Near Ernakulam]	Kerala	Namm Alvar
95	Thirumozhikkalam [Near Cochin airport]	Kerala	Namm Alvar, Thirumangai Alvar
96	Thiruvittuvakodu [Near Trichur]	Kerala	Kulashekar Alvar
97	Thirunavai [Near Kuttipuram]	Kerala	Namm Alvar, Thirumangai Alvar
98	Thirudwaraka	Gujarat	Peri Alvar, Andal, Thirumangai Alvar
99	Thiruayodhya	UP	Kulashekar Alvar
100	Thirunaimisaranyam	UP	Thirumangai Alvar
101	Thiruvaipadi [Ayarpadi]	UP	Peri Alvar, Andal, Thirumangai Alvar
102	Thiruvadamathura [Govardhaneshan]	UP	Peri Alvar, Andal, Thondaripudi Alvar, Thirumangai Alvar, Namm Alvar
103	Thirukkandam [Devaprayag]	Uttarakhand	Peri Alvar
104	Thiruppirudi [Jyoshimutt]	Uttarakhand	Thirumangai Alvar

105	Thiruvadari asram [Badarinath]	Uttarakhand	Peri Alvar, Thirumangai Alvar
106	Thirusaligramam	Nepal	Thirumangai Alvar,Peri Alvar
107	Thiruparkadal [Milk ocean]		Peri Alvar, Andal, Kulashekar Alvar, Thirumalishai Alvar, Thondaripudi Alvar, Thirumangai Alvar, Poigai Alvar, Boothath Alvar, Pei Alvar, Namm Alvar
108	Thiruparamapadam		Peri Alvar, Andal, Thirumalishai Alvar, Thirupann Alvar, Thirumangai Alvar, Poigai Alvar, , Pei Alvar, Namm Alvar